Anonymous

Comparison of the Customs Law of 1883 with the New Law

of 1890

With index, to which is appended the Administrative customs law of 1890

Anonymous

Comparison of the Customs Law of 1883 with the New Law of 1890
With index, to which is appended the Administrative customs law of 1890

ISBN/EAN: 9783337429331

Printed in Europe, USA, Canada, Australia, Japan

Cover: Foto ©Suzi / pixelio.de

More available books at **www.hansebooks.com**

COMPARISON

OF THE

CUSTOMS LAW OF 1883

WITH THE

NEW LAW OF 1890,

WITH INDEX,

TO WHICH IS APPENDED

THE ADMINISTRATIVE CUSTOMS LAW OF 1890

Prepared under the direction of the Committee on Finance, United States Senate, in accordance with Senate Resolution of December 5, 1890.

————— ◄ ► —————

WASHINGTON:
GOVERNMENT PRINTING OFFICE.
1890.

INDEX TO SCHEDULES.

3

INDEX.

A.

5

Paragraph.

Knives—Continued.
pocket 165
table 167
Knots, metal 196
Kryolith................................... 550
Kyanite 625

L.

Lac—
spirits 627
sulphur 727
Lac dye—
button, crude, seed, shell, stick ... 626
Lace window-curtains, cotton 373
Laces—
cotton 373
flax 373
for hats, bonnets, and hoods.. 518
linen 373
metal 196
silk 413
wool 398
Lactarine.................................. 628
Lahn 737
Lambskins................................. 456
Lame 737
Lampblack 52
Lance-wood 756
Lard 314
Last blocks 223
Lastings 428
Laths..................................... 224
Laudanum.................................. 47
Lava 629
Lead 199, 200, 201
acetate of................................. 62
articles of................................ 215
dross 199
nitrate of 64
ore 199
products 62–67
red 66
type-metal................................. 208
white...................................... 67
Leaf—
bronze or Dutch metal........ 190
gold 197
silver 198
tobacco 242
Leather...............................455–461
bend or belting 455
manufactures of...............455–458
book-binders' calf-skin 456
boots and shoes 456
calf-skins 455
chamois skins 456
for uppers or vamps 457
gloves 458
japanned calf-skin 456
kangaroo skins............................. 456
manufactures............455–457, 461
morocco 456
sheep and goat skins........... 456
sole 455
Leaves.................................24, 560
Leeches 630
Lees crystals.............................. 91
Lemon—
grass oil.................................. 661

Paragraph.

Lemon—Continued.
juice 631
oil 661
peel 305
Lemons 301
Lemonade.................................. 340
Lenses 120, 121, 591
Letter-press copying paper......... 422
Libraries or parts of.............. 516
Library, Congressional............ 514
Lichens 24, 560
Licorice—
juice 33
paste or roll.............................. 33
root....................................... 632
Life—
boats 633
saving apparatus........................... 633
Lignum vitæ............................... 756
Lily of the valley........................ 666
Lime.. 96
borate of.................................. 14
chloride of................................ 635
citrate of................................. 634
juice 631
sulphate 680
Limes...................................... 301
oil of..................................... 661
Limestone 127, 128
Linen—
brown and bleached 350
cloth...................................... 371
collars and cuffs 372
embroideries 373
hemstitched handkerchiefs.... 373
hydraulic hose 368
insertings 373
laces 373
manufactures of, embroidered 373
neck rufflings............................. 373
Linoleum 369
Linseed 285
oil 41
Liquors 330, 332, 336
Literary societies and institutions.515, 692
Litharge 63
Lithographic stones 636
prints.................................420, 515
Lithographs 420
Litmus 637
Loadstones................................. 638
Logs....................................... 754
Logwood extracts 26
Longitudinal ribs for fence wire... 147
Looking-glass plates............ 117
Lumber 218, 220
lumber, hardwood............ 220
for vessels. Sec. 8.

M.

Macaroni 258
Mace....................................... 717
oil 661
Machinery for repair. Sec. 14.
Patterns................................... 652
Mackerel 292
Madder 639
Indian 639

19

AN ACT to reduce the revenue and equalize duties on imports, and for other purposes.

Be it enacted by the Senate and House of Representatives of the United States of America in Congress assembled, That on and after the sixth day of October, eighteen hundred and ninety, unless otherwise specially provided for in this act, there shall be levied, collected, and paid upon all articles imported from foreign countries, and mentioned in the schedules herein contained, the rates of duty which are, by the schedules and paragraphs, respectively prescribed, namely :

[All changes from the old law are indicated by foot-notes or by italics.]

SCHEDULE A.—CHEMICALS, OILS AND PAINTS.

ACIDS.—

1. Acetic or pyroligneous acid, not exceeding the specific gravity of one and forty-seven one-thousandths, one and one-half cents per pound ; exceeding the specific gravity of one and forty-seven one thousandths, four cents per pound.
   Old law: Two cents and four cents.
2. Boracic acid, five cents per pound.
   Old law: Pure, five cents per pound; commercial, four cents.
3. Chromic acid, six cents per pound.
   Old law: Fifteen per centum.
4. Citric acid, ten cents per pound.
5. Sulphuric acid or oil of vitriol, not otherwise specially provided for, one-fourth of one cent per pound.
   Old law: Free under general provision for acids.
6. Tannic acid or tannin, seventy-five cents per pound.
   Old law: One dollar per pound.
7. Tartaric acid, ten cents per pound.
8. Alcoholic perfumery, including cologne-water and other toilet waters, two dollars per gallon and fifty per centum ad valorem ; alcoholic compounds not specially provided for in this act, two dollars per gallon and twenty-five per centum ad valorem.
9. Alumina, alum, alum cake, patent alum, sulphate of alumina, and aluminous cake, and alum in crystals or ground, six-tenths of one cent per pound.
10. AMMONIA.—Carbonate of, one and three-fourths cents per pound; muriate of, or sal-ammoniac, three-fourths of one cent per pound; sulphate of, one-half of one cent per pound.
    Old law: Carbonate of, twenty per centum; muriate of, ten per centum; sulphate of, twenty per centum.
11. Blacking of all kinds, twenty-five per centum ad valorem.
12. Blue vitriol, or sulphate of copper, two cents per pound.
    Old law: Three cents per pound.

27:

13. Bone-char, suitable for use in decolorizing sugars, twenty-five per centum ad valorem.

   Old law: All bone-char twenty-five per centum.

14. Borax, crude, or borate of soda, or borate of lime, three cents per pound; refined borax, five cents per pound.

15. Camphor, refined, four cents per pound.

   Old law: Five cents per pound.

16. Chalk, prepared, precipitated, French, and red, one cent per pound; all other chalk preparations not specially provided for in this act, twenty per centum ad valorem.

17. Chloroform, twenty-five cents per pound.

   Old law: Fifty cents per pound.

COAL-TAR PREPARATIONS.—

18. All coal-tar colors or dyes, by whatever name known, and not specially provided for in this act, thirty-five per centum ad valorem.

19. All preparations of coal-tar, not colors or dyes, not specially provided for in this act, twenty per centum ad valorem.

20. Cobalt, oxide of, thirty cents per pound.

   Old law: Twenty per centum.

21. Collodion and all compounds of pyroxyline, by whatever name known, fifty cents per pound; rolled or in sheets, but not made up into articles, sixty cents per pound; if in finished or partly-finished articles, sixty cents per pound and twenty-five per centum ad valorem.

22. Coloring for brandy, wine, beer, or other liquors, fifty per centum ad valorem.

   Text of old law : Coloring for brandy, 50 per centum.

23. Copperas or sulphate of iron, three-tenths of one cent per pound.

24. Drugs, such as barks, beans, berries, balsams, buds, bulbs, and bulbous roots, and excrescences, such as nut-galls, fruits, flowers, dried fibers grains, gums, and gum resins, herbs, leaves, lichens, mosses, nuts, roots and stems, spices, vegetables, seeds (aromatic, not garden seeds), and seeds of morbid growth, weeds, woods used expressly for dyeing, and dried insects, any of the foregoing which are not edible, but which have been advanced in value or condition by refining or grinding, or by other process of manufacture, and not specially provided for in this act, ten per centum ad valorem.

25. Ethers sulphuric, forty cents per pound ; spirits of nitrous ether, twenty-five cents per pound ; fruit ethers, oils, or essences, two dollars and fifty cents per pound ; ethers of all kinds not specially provided for in this act, one dollar per pound.

   Old law: Ethers sulphuric, fifty cents per pound; nitrous ether, thirty cents per pound; ethers all other, one dollar per pound; œnanthic, or oil of cognac, four dollars per ounce; fruit ethers, etc., two dollars and fifty cents per pound; oil or essence of rum, fifty cents per ounce.

26. Extracts and decoctions of logwood and other dye-woods, extract of sumac, and extracts of barks, such as are commonly used for dyeing or tanning, not specially provided for in this act, seven-eighths of one cent per pound; extracts of hemlock bark one-half of one cent per pound.

   Old law: Logwood and other dye-woods, extract, ten per centum; sumac extract, twenty per centum; extract of hemlock and other barks for tanning, twenty per centum.

27. Gelatine, glue, and isinglass or fish-glue, valued at not above seven cents per pound, one and one-half cents per pound ; valued at above seven cents per pound and not above thirty cents per pound, twenty-five per centum ad valorem ; valued at above thirty cents per pound, thirty per centum ad valorem.

> Old law: Glue, twenty per centum; gelatine, thirty per centum; fish-glue, or isinglass, twenty-five per centum.

28. Glycerine, crude, not purified, one and three-fourths cents per pound. Refined, four and one-half cents per pound. .

> Old law: Crude, two cents per pound; refined, five cents pound.

29. Indigo, extracts, or pastes of, three-fourths of one cent per pound ; carmined, ten cents per pound.

> Old law: All ten per centum.

30. Ink and ink-powders, printers' ink, and all other ink, not specially provided for in this act, thirty per centum ad valorem.

> Old law: Ink of all kinds and ink powders, thirty per centum.

31. Iodine, resublimed, thirty cents per pound.

32. Iodoform, one dollar and fifty cents per pound.

> Old law: Two dollars per pound.

33. Licorice, extracts of, in paste, rolls, or other forms, five and one-half cents per pound.

> Old law: Paste or roll, seven and one-half cents per pound; juice, three cents pound.

34. Magnesia, carbonate of, medicinal, four cents per pound : calcined, eight cents per pound ; sulphate of, or Epsom salts, three-tenths of one cent per pound.

> Old law: Carbonate of, five cents per pound; calcined, ten cents per pound; sulphate, twelve cents per pound.

35. Morphia, or morphine, and all salts thereof, fifty cents per ounce.

> Old law: One dollar per pound.

OILS.—

36. Alizarine assistant, or soluble oil, or oleate of soda, or Turkey red oil, containing fifty per centum or more of castor oil, eighty cents per gallon; containing less than fifty per centum of castor oil, forty cents per gallon; all other, thirty per centum ad valorem.

> Old law: By ruling of Treasury Department as castor oil at eighty cents per gallon.

37. Castor oil, eighty cents per gallon.

38. Cod-liver oil, fifteen cents per gallon.

> Old law: Twenty-five per centum.

39. Cotton-seed oil, ten cents per gallon of seven and one-half pounds weight.

> Old law: Twenty-five cents per gallon

40. Croton oil, thirty cents per pound.

> Old law: Fifty cents per pound.

41. Flaxseed or linseed and poppy-seed oil, raw, boiled, or oxidized, thirty-two cents per gallon of seven and one-half pounds weight.

> Old law: Twenty-five cents per gallon; poppy oil free.

42. Fusel oil, or amylic alcohol, ten per centum ad valorem

43. Hemp-seed oil and rape-seed oil, ten cents per gallon.

44. Olive oil, fit for salad purposes, thirty-five cents per gallon.
Old law: Twenty-five per centum.

45. Peppermint oil, eighty cents per pound.
Old law: Twenty-five per centum.

46. Seal, herring, whale, and other fish oil not specially provided for in this act, eight cents per gallon.
Old law: Twenty-five per centum.

47. Opium, aqueous extract of, for medicinal uses, and tincture of, as laudanum, and all other liquid preparations of opium, not specially provided for in this act, forty per centum ad valorem.

48. Opium containing less than nine per centum of morphia, and opium prepared for smoking, twelve dollars per pound; but opium prepared for smoking and other preparations of opium deposited in bonded-warehouse shall not be removed therefrom without payment of duties, and such duties shall not be refunded.
Old law: Ten dollars per pound on opium for smoking; containing less than nine per centum of opium prohibited; opium, crude, containing nine per centum or more one dollar per pound.

PAINTS, COLORS, AND VARNISHES.—

49. Baryta, sulphate of, or barytes, including barytes earth, unmanufactured, one dollar and twelve cents per ton; manufactured, six dollars and seventy-two cents per ton.
Old law: Unmanufactured ten per centum; manufactured, one-quarter cent per pound.

50. Blues, such as Berlin, Prussian, Chinese, and all others, containing ferrocyanide of iron, dry or ground in or mixed with oil, six cents per pound; in pulp, or mixed with water six cents per pound on the material contained therein when dry.
Old law: Twenty per centum.

51. Blanc-fixe, or satin white, or artificial sulphate of barytes, three-fourths of one cent per pound.
Old law: Twenty-five per centum.

52. Black, made from bone, ivory, or vegetable, under whatever name known, including bone-black and lamp-black, dry or ground in oil or water, twenty-five per centum ad valorem.
Old law: Change in text, but same rate.

53. Chrome yellow, chrome green, and all other chromium colors in which lead and bichromate of potash or soda are component parts, dry, or ground in or mixed with oil, four and one-half cents per pound; in pulp or mixed with water, four and one-half cents per pound on the material contained therein when dry.
Old law: Twenty-five per centum.

54. Ocher and ochery earths, sienna and sienna earths, umber and umber earths not specially provided for in this act, dry, one-fourth of one cent per pound; ground in oil, one and one-half cents per pound.
Old law: Dry, one-half cent per pound: in oil, one cent per pound.

55 Ultramarine blue, four and one-half cents per pound.
Old law: Five cents per pound.

56. Varnishes, including so-called gold size or japan, thirty-five per centum ad valorem ; and on spirit varnishes for the alcohol contained therein, one dollar and thirty-two cents per gallon additional.
Old law: Forty per centum ad valorem on varnish; gold size, free; Japan, forty per centum by Treasury ruling.

57. Vermilion red, and colors containing quicksilver, dry or ground in oil or water, twelve cents per pound.
 Old law: Twenty-five per centum.

58. Wash blue, containing ultramarine, three cents per pound.
 Old law: Twenty per centum.

59. Whiting and Paris white, dry, one-half of one cent per pound ; ground in oil, or putty, one cent per pound.

60. Zinc, oxide of, *and while paint containing zinc, but not containing lead ;* dry, one and one-fourth cents per pound ; ground in oil, one and three-fourth cents per pound.
 NOTE.—New matter in italics.

61. All other paints and colors, whether dry or mixed, or ground in water or oil, including lakes, crayons, smalts, and frostings, not specially provided for in this act, and artists' colors of all kinds, in tubes or otherwise, twenty-five per centum ad valorem; all paints and colors, mixed or ground with water or solutions other than oil, and commercially known as artists' water color paints, thirty per centum ad valorem.
 Old law· Twenty-five per centum on all. Entire change of text.

LEAD PRODUCTS.—

62. Acetate of lead, white, five and one-half cents per pound · brown, three and one-half cents per pound.

63. Litharge, three cents per pound.

64. Nitrate of lead, three cents per pound.

65. Orange mineral, three and one-half cents per pound.
 Old law: Three cents per pound.

66. Red lead, three cents per pound.
 NOTE.—New matter in italics.

67. White lead, *and white paint containing lead,* dry or in pulp, or ground or mixed with oil, three cents per pound.
 NOTE.—New matter in italics.

68. Phosphorus, twenty cents per pound.
 Old law: Ten cents per pound.

POTASH.—

69. Bichromate and chromate of, three cents per pound.

70. Caustic or hydrate of, refined in sticks or rolls, one cent per pound.
 Old law: Twenty per centum.

71. Hydriodate, iodide, and iodate of, fifty cents per pound.

72. Nitrate of, or saltpeter, refined, one cent per pound.
 Old law: One and one-half cents per pound.

73. Prussiate of, red, ten cents per pound ; yellow, five cents per pound.

PREPARATIONS.—

74. All medicinal preparations, including medicinal proprietary preparations, of which alcohol is a component part, or in the preparation of which alcohol is used, not specially provided for in this act, fifty cents per pound.
 Old law: Change of text. Hoffman's anodyne, thirty cents per pound.

75. All medicinal preparations, including medicinal proprietary preparations, of which alcohol is not a component part, and not specially provided for in this act, twenty-five per centum

ad valorem ; calomel and other mercurial medicinal preparations, thirty-five per centum ad valorem.

Old law: Twenty-five per centum and fifty per centum.

76. Products or preparations known as alkalies, alkaloids, distilled oils, essential oils, expressed oils, rendered oils, and all combinations of the foregoing, and all chemical compounds and salts, not specially provided for in this act, twenty-five per centum ad valorem.

77. Preparations used as applications to the hair, mouth, teeth, or skin, such as cosmetics, dentifrices, pastes, pomades, powders, and tonics, including all known as toilet preparations, not specially provided for in this act, fifty per centum ad valorem.

Change of text.

78. Santonine, and all salts thereof containing eighty per centum or over of santonine, two dollars and fifty cents per pound.

Old law: Three dollars per pound.

79. Soap: Castile-soap, one and one-fourth cents per pound; fancy, perfumed, and all descriptions of toilet-soap, fifteen cents per pound; all other soaps, not specially provided for in this act, twenty per centum ad valorem.

Old law: Castile-soap, twenty per centum.

SODA.—

80. Bicarbonate of soda or supercarbonate of soda or saleratus, one cent per pound.

Old law: One and one-half cents per pound.

81. Hydrate of, or caustic soda, one cent per pound.

82. Bichromate and chromate of, three cents per pound.

Old law: Not enumerated, but classified under bichromate of potash at three cents per pound.

83. Sal-soda, or soda-crystals, and soda-ash, one fourth of one cent per pound.

84. Silicate of soda, or other alkaline silicate, one-half of one cent per pound.

85. Sulphate of soda, or salt-cake or niter-cake, one dollar and twenty-five cents per ton.

Old law: Twenty per centum.

86. Sponges, twenty per centum ad valorem.

87. Strychnia, or strychnine, and all salts thereof, forty cents per ounce.

Old law: Fifty cents per ounce.

88. Sulphur, refined, eight dollars per ton; sublimed, or flowers of, ten dollars per ton.

Old law: Refined, ten dollars per ton; flowers, twenty dollars per ton.

89. Sumac, ground, four-tenths of one cent per pound.

Old law: Three-tenths cent per pound.

90. Tartar, cream of, and patent tartar, six cents per pound.

91. Tartars and lees crystals, partly refined, four cents per pound.

92. Tartrate of soda and potassa, or Rochelle salts, three cents per pound.

SCHEDULE B.—EARTHS, EARTHENWARE, AND GLASSWARE.

BRICK AND TILE—

93. Fire-brick, not glazed, enameled, ornamented, or decorated in any manner, one dollar and twenty-five cents per ton; glazed, enameled, ornamented, or decorated, forty-five per centum ad valorem.

> Old law: Fire-brick, twenty per centum; brick, twenty-five per centum.

94. Tiles and brick, other than fire-brick, not glazed, ornamented, painted, enameled, vitrified, or decorated, twenty-five per centum ad valorem; ornamented, glazed, painted, enameled, vitrified, or decorated, and all encaustic, forty-five per centum ad valorem.

> Old law: Encaustic tiles, thirty-five per centum; roofing and paving tiles, twenty per centum, and some classed by Treasury rulings as placques, etc., at sixty per centum.

CEMENT, LIME, AND PLASTER—

95. Roman, Portland, and other hydraulic cement, in barrels, sacks, or other packages, eight cents per one hundred pounds, including weight of barrel or package; in bulk, seven cents per one hundred pounds; other cement, twenty per centum ad valorem.

> Old law: Twenty per centum.

96. Lime, six cents per one hundred pounds, including weight of barrel or package.

> Old law: Ten per centum.

97. Plaster of Paris, or gypsum, ground, one dollar per ton; calcined, one dollar and seventy-five cents per ton.

> Old law; Twenty per centum.

CLAYS OR EARTHS—

98. Clays or earths, unwrought or unmanufactured, not specially provided for in this act, one dollar and fifty cents per ton ; wrought or manufactured, not specially provided for in this act, three dollars per ton; china clay, or kaolin, three dollars per ton.

EARTHENWARE AND CHINA—

99. Common brown earthenware, common stoneware, and crucibles, not ornamented or decorated in any manner, twenty-five per centum ad valorem.

> Old law: Stoneware above the capacity of ten gallons, twenty per centum; crucibles, twenty-five per centum.

100. China, porcelain, parian, bisque, earthen, stone and crockery ware, including placques, ornaments, toys, charms, vases, and statuettes, painted, tinted, stained, enameled, printed, gilded, or otherwise decorated or ornamented in any manner, sixty per centum ad valorem; if plain white, and not ornamented or decorated in any manner, fifty-five per centum ad valorem.

> NOTE.—The text is made more comprehensive than in the old law.

101. All other china, porcelain, parian, bisque, earthen, stone, and crockery ware, and manufactures of the same, by whatsoever designation or name known in the trade, including lava tips for burners, not specially provided for in this act, if

ornamented or decorated in any manner, sixty per centum ad valorem; if not ornamented or decorated, fifty-five per centum ad valorem.

Old law: Fifty-five per centum.

102. Gas-retorts, three dollars each.

Old law: Twenty-five per centum.

GLASS AND GLASSWARE—

103. Green, and colored, molded or pressed, and flint, and lime glass bottles, holding more than one pint, and demijohns, and carboys (covered or uncovered), and other molded or pressed green and colored and flint or lime bottle glassware, not specially provided for in this act, one cent per pound. Green, and colored, molded or pressed, and flint, and lime glass bottles, and vials holding not more than one pint and not less than one-quarter of a pint, one and one-half cents per pound; if holding less than one-fourth of a pint, fifty cents per gross.

Old law: Green and colored, one cent per pound; flint and lime, forty per centum.

104. All articles enumerated in the preceding paragraph, if filled, and not otherwise provided for in this act, and the contents are subject to an ad valorem rate of duty, or to a rate of duty based upon the value, the value of such bottles, vials, or other vessels shall be added to the value of the contents for the ascertainment of the dutiable value of the latter; but if filled, and not otherwise provided for in this act, and the contents are not subject to an ad valorem rate of duty, or to rate of duty based on the value, or are free of duty, such bottles, vials, or other vessels shall pay, in addition to the duty, if any, on their contents, the rates of duty prescribed in the preceding paragraph: *Provided*, That no article manufactured from glass described in the preceding paragraph shall pay a less rate of duty than forty per centum ad valorem.

Old law: Green and colored thirty per centum; flint and lime forty per centum, in addition to duty on contents.

105. Flint and lime, pressed glassware, not cut, engraved, painted, etched, decorated, colored, printed, stained, silvered, or gilded, sixty per centum ad valorem.

Old law: Forty per centum.

106. All articles of glass, cut, engraved, painted, colored, printed, stained, decorated, silvered, or gilded, not including plate glass silvered, or looking-glass plates, sixty per centum ad valorem.

Old law: forty-five per centum.

107. Chemical glassware *for use in laboratory, and not otherwise specially provided for in this act*, forty-five per centum ad valorem.

Note.—New matter in italics.

108. Thin-blown glass, blown with or without a mold, including glass chimneys and all other manufactures of glass, or of which glass shall be the component material of chief value, not specially provided for in this act, sixty per centum ad valorem.

Old law: Mostly forty and forty-five per centum.

109. Heavy-blown glass, blown with or without a mold, not cut or decorated, finished or unfinished, sixty per centum ad valorem.

Old law: Forty per centum.

110. Porcelain or opal glassware, sixty per centum ad valorem.

Old law: Forty per centum.

111. All cut, engraved, painted, or otherwise ornamented or decorated glass bottles, decanters, or other vessels of glass shall, if filled, pay duty in addition to any duty chargeable on the contents, as if not filled, unless otherwise specially provided for in this act.

112. Unpolished cylinder, crown, and common window-glass, not exceeding ten by fifteen inches square, one and three-eighths cents per pound; above that, and not exceeding sixteen by twenty-four inches square, one and seven-eighths cents per pound; above that, and not exceeding twenty-four by thirty inches square, two and three-eighths cents per pound; above that, and not exceeding twenty-four by thirty-six inches square, two and seven-eighths cents per pound; all above that, three and one-eighth cents per pound: *Provided,* That unpolished cylinder, crown and common window glass, imported in boxes, shall contain fifty square feet, as nearly as sizes will permit, and the duty shall be computed thereon according to the actual weight of glass.

Old law: To ten by fifteen, one and three-eighths cents per pound; above that to sixteen by twenty-four, one and seven-eighths; above that to twenty-four by thirty, two and three-eighths; all above, two and seven-eighths, with an allowance for box weight on single thick of five pounds, and on double thick of ten pounds.

113. Cylinder and crown-glass, polished, not exceeding sixteen by twenty-four inches square, four cents per square foot; above that, and not exceeding twenty-four by thirty inches square, six cents per square foot; above that, and not exceeding twenty-four by sixty inches square, twenty cents per square foot; above that, forty cents per square foot.

Old law: To ten by fifteen, two and one-half cents square foot; above that to sixteen by twenty-four, four cents; above that to twenty-four by thirty, six cents: above that to twenty-four by sixty, twenty cents; all above that, forty cents.

114. Fluted, rolled, or rough plate-glass, not including crown, cylinder, or common window-glass, not exceeding ten by fifteen inches square three-fourths of one cent per square foot; above that, and not exceeding sixteen by twenty-four inches square, one cent per square foot; above that, and not exceeding twenty-four by thirty inches square, one and one-half cents per square foot; all above that, two cents per square foot; and all fluted, rolled, or rough plate-glass, weighing over one hundred pounds per one hundred square feet, shall pay an additional duty on the excess at the same rates herein imposed: *Provided, That all of the above plate-glass when ground, smoothed or otherwise obscured shall be subject to the same rate of duty as cast polished plate-glass unsilvered.*

Old law: Was the same, omitting the proviso. New matter in italics.

115. Cast polished plate-glass, *finished or unfinished* and unsilvered, not exceeding sixteen by twenty-four inches square, five cents per square foot; above that, and not exceeding twenty-four by thirty inches square, eight cents per square foot; above that, and not exceeding twenty-four by sixty inches square, twenty-five cents per square foot; all above that, fifty cents per square foot.

> Old law: In addition to above had a bracket not exceeding ten by fifteen at three cents per square foot, but did not contain the words " finished or unfinished."

116. Cast polished plate-glass, silvered, and looking-glass plates, not exceeding sixteen by twenty-four inches square, six cents per square foot; above that, and not exceeding twenty-four by thirty inches square, ten cents per square foot; above that, and not exceeding twenty-four by sixty inches square, thirty-five cents per square foot; all above that, sixty cents per square foot.

> Old law has a bracket up to ten by fifteen at four cents per square foot.

117. But no looking-glass plates, or plate-glass silvered, when framed, shall pay a less rate of duty than that imposed upon similar glass of like description not framed, but shall pay in addition thereto upon such frames the rate of duty applicable thereto when imported separate.

> Old law: Additional duty of thirty per centum on the frames.

118. Cast polished plate-glass, silvered or unsilvered, and cylinder, crown, or common window-glass, when ground, obscured, frosted, sanded, enameled, beveled, etched, embossed, engraved, stained, colored, or otherwise ornamented or decorated, shall be subject to a duty of ten per centum ad valorem in addition to the rates otherwise chargeable thereon.

> Not in old law.

119. Spectacles and eyeglasses, or spectacles and eyeglass-frames, sixty per centum ad valorem.

> Old law: Forty-five per centum or twenty-five per centum or according to component of chief value.

120. On lenses costing one dollar and fifty cents per gross pairs, or less, sixty per centum ad valorem.

> Old law: Forty-five per centum.

121. Spectacle and eyeglass lenses with their edges ground or beveled to fit frames, sixty per centum ad valorem.

> Old law: Forty-five per centum or free.

122. All stained or painted window-glass and stained or painted glass windows, and hand, pocket, or table mirrors not exceeding in size one hundred and forty-four square inches, with or without frames or cases, of whatever material composed, lenses of glass or pebble, wholly or partly manufactured, and not specially provided for in this act, and fusible enamel, forty-five per centum ad valorem.

> Old law: Forty-five per centum, thirty per centum, ten per centum.

MARBLE AND STONE, AND MANUFACTURES OF—

123. Marble of all kinds in block, rough or squared, sixty-five cents per cubic foot.

124. **Veined marble, sawed,** dressed, **or otherwise, including marble** slabs and marble paving-tiles, one dollar and ten cents
per cubic foot (but in measurement no slab shall be computed at less than one inch in thickness).

Old law does not contain the words in parenthesis.

125. Manufactures of marble not specially provided for in this
act, fifty per centum ad valorem.

STONE—

126. Burr-stones manufactured or bound up into mill-stones, fifteen per centum ad valorem.

Old law: Twenty per centum.

127. Freestone, granite, sandstone, limestone, and other building
or monumental stone, except marble, unmanufactured or
undressed, not specially provided for in this act, eleven
cents per cubic foot.

Old law: One dollar per ton.

128. Freestone, granite, sandstone, limestone, and other building
or monumental stone, except marble, not specially provided
for in this act, hewn, dressed, or polished, forty per centum
ad valorem.

Old law: Twenty per centum.

129. Grindstones, finished or unfinished, one dollar and seventy-
five cents per ton.

SLATE—

130. Slates, slate chimney-pieces, mantels, slabs for tables, and all
other manufactures of slate, not specially provided for in
this act, thirty per centum ad valorem.

131. Roofing slates, twenty-five per centum ad valorem.

SCHEDULE C.—METALS AND MANUFACTURES OF.

IRON AND STEEL.

132. Chromate of iron, or chromic ore, fifteen per centum ad
valorem.

133. Iron ore. including manganiferous iron ore, also the dross or
residuum from burnt pyrites, seventy-five cents per ton. Sulphur
ore, as pyrites, or sulphuret of iron in its natural state, containing
not more than three and one-half per centum copper, seventy-five
cents per ton : *Provided,* That ore containing more than two per
centum of copper shall pay, in addition thereto, one-half of one
cent per pound for the copper contained therein : *Provided, also,
That sulphur ore as pyrites or sulphuret of iron in its natural state,
containing in excess of twenty-five per centum of sulphur, shall be
free of duty, except on the copper contained therein, as above provided: And provided further, That in levying and collecting the duty
on iron ore no deduction shall be made from the weight of the ore on
account of moisture which may be chemically or physically combined therewith.*

Old law: The copper was dutiable at two and one-half cents per
pound. The last two provisos are new matter.

134. Iron in pigs, iron kentledge, spiegeleisen, ferro-manganese,
ferro-silicon, wrought and cast scrap iron, and scrap steel, three-

tenths of one cent per pound; but nothing shall be deemed scrap iron or scrap steel except waste or refuse iron or steel fit only to be remanufactured.

Old law: Did not contain ferro manganese or ferro silicon. The scrap iron was confined to that which had been in actual use.

135. Bar-iron, rolled or hammered, comprising flats not less than one inch wide, nor less than three-eighths of one inch thick, eight-tenths of one cent per pound; round iron not less than three-fourths of one inch in diameter, and square iron not less than three-fourths of one inch square, nine-tenths of one cent per pound; flats less than one inch wide, or less than three-eighths of one inch thick; round iron less than three-fourths of one inch and not less than seven-sixteenths of one inch in diameter; and square iron less than three-fourths of one inch square, one cent per pound.

Old law: The respective rates were eight-tenths cent per pound, one cent per pound, one and one-tenth cents per pound.

136. Round iron, in coils or rods, less than seven-sixteenths of one inch in diameter, and bars or shapes of rolled iron, not specially provided for in this act, one and one-tenth cents per pound : *Provided*, That all iron in slabs, blooms, loops, or other forms less finished than iron in bars, and more advanced than pig-iron, except castings, shall be rated as iron in bars, and be subject to a duty of eight-tenths of one cent per pound; and none of the iron above enumerated in this paragraph shall pay a less rate of duty than thirty-five per centum ad valorem : *Provided further*, That all iron bars, blooms, billets, or sizes or shapes of any kind, in the manufacture of which charcoal is used as fuel, shall be subject to a duty of not less than twenty-two dollars per ton.

Old law: One and two-tenths cent per pound.

137. Beams, girders, joists, angles, channels, car-truck channels, T T, columns and posts or parts or sections of columns and posts, deck and bulb beams, and building forms, together with all other structural shapes of iron or steel, whether plain or punched, or fitted for use, nine-tenths of one cent per pound.

Old law: One and one-fourth cents per pound.

138. Boiler or other plate iron or steel, except saw-plates hereinafter provided for, not thinner than number ten wire gauge, sheared or unsheared, and skelp iron or steel sheared or rolled in grooves, valued at one cent per pound or less, five-tenths of one cent per pound; valued above one cent and not above one and four-tenths cents per pound, sixty-five hundredths of one cent per pound; valued above one and four tenths cents and not above two cents per pound, eight tenths of one cent per pound; valued above two cents and not above three cents per pound, one and one-tenth cents per pound; valued above three cents and not above four cents per pound, one and five-tenths cents per pound; valued above four cents and not above seven cents per pound, two cents per pound; valued above seven cents and not above ten cents per pound, two and eight-tenths cents per pound; valued above ten cents and not above thirteen cents per pound, three and one-half cents per pound; valued above thirteen cents per pound, forty-five per centum ad valorem: *Provided*, That all plate iron or steel thinner than number ten wire gauge shall pay duty as iron or steel sheets.

Old law: Boiler or other plate iron, one and one-fourth cents per pound if iron; forty-five per centum if steel.

139. Forgings of iron or steel, or forged iron and steel combined, of whatever shape, or in whatever stage of manufacture, not specially provided for in this act, two and three-tenths cents per pound: *Provided,* That no forgings of iron or steel, or forgings of iron and steel combined, by whatever process made, shall pay a less rate of duty than forty-five per centum ad valorem.

> Old law : Forgings of iron and steel, or forged iron, of whatever shape, or in whatever stage of manufacture, not specially enumerated or provided for in this act, two and one-half cents per pound.

140. Hoop, or band, or scroll, or other iron or steel, valued at three cents per pound or less, eight inches or less in width, and less than three-eighths of one inch thick and not thinner than number ten wire gauge, one cent per pound; thinner than number ten wire gauge and not thinner than number twenty wire gauge, one and one-tenth cents per pound; thinner than number twenty wire gauge, one and three-tenths cents per pound: *Provided,* That hoop or band iron, or hoop or band steel, cut to length, or wholly or partially manufactured into hoops or ties for baling purposes, barrel hoops of iron or steel, and hoop or band iron or hoop or band steel flared, splayed or punched, with or without buckles or fastenings, shall pay two-tenths of one cent per pound more duty than that imposed on the hoop or band iron or steel from which they are made.

> Old law : Hoop, or band, or scroll, or other iron, eight inches or less in width, and not thinner than number ten wire gauge, one cent per pound ; thinner than number ten wire gauge, and not thinner than number twenty wire gauge, one and two-tenths of one cent per pound ; thinner than number twenty wire gauge, one and four tenths of one cent per pound: *Provided,* That all articles not specially enumerated or provided for in this act, whether wholly or partly manufactured, made from sheet, plate, hoop, band or scroll iron herein provided for, or of which such sheet, plate, hoop, band, or scroll iron shall be the material of chief value, shall pay one-fourth of one cent per pound more duty than that imposed on the iron from which they are made, or which shall be such material of chief value.
>
> If steel, forty-five per centum: Iron and steel cotton-ties, or hoops for bailing purposes, not thinner than number twenty wire gauge, thirty-five per centum ad valorem.
>
> If steel, forty-five per centum: Sheet iron, common or black, thinner than one inch and one-half and not thinner than number twenty wire gauge, one and one-tenth of one cent per pound; thinner than number twenty wire gauge and not thinner than number twenty-five wire gauge, one and two-tenths of one cent per pound; thinner than number twenty-five wire gauge and not thinner than number twenty-nine wire gauge, one and five-tenths of one cent per pound; thinner than number twenty-nine wire gauge, and all iron commercially known as common or black taggers iron, whether put up in boxes or bundles or not, thirty per centum ad valorem.

141. Railway-bars, made of iron or steel, and railway-bars made in part of steel, **T**-rails, and punched iron or steel flat rails, six-tenths of one cent per pound.

> Old law : Iron or steel tee rails, weighing not over twenty-five pounds to the yard, nine-tenths of one cent per pound; iron or steel flat rails, punched, eight-tenths of one cent per pound.
>
> Iron railway bars, weighing more than twenty-five pounds to the yard, seven-tenths of one cent per pound.
>
> Steel railway-bars and railway bars made in part of steel, weighing more than twenty-five pounds to the yard, seventeen dollars per ton.

142. Sheets of iron or steel, common or black, including all iron or steel commercially known as common or black taggers iron or steel, and skelp iron or steel, valued at three cents per pound or less: Thinner than number ten and not thinner than number twenty wire gauge, one cent per pound; thinner than number twenty wire gauge, and not thinner than number twenty-five wire gauge, one and one-tenth cents per pound ; thinner than number twenty-five wire gauge, one and four-tenths cents per pound; corrugated or crimped, one and four-tenths cents per pound: *Provided*, That all common or black sheet-iron or sheet-steel not thinner than number ten wire gauge shall pay duty as plate iron or plate steel.

> Old law : Sheet iron, common or black, thinner than one inch and one-half and not thinner than number twenty wire gauge, one and one-tenth of one cent per pound ; thinner than number twenty wire gauge and not thinner than number twenty-five wire gauge, one and two-tenths of one cent per pound ; thinner than number twenty-five wire gauge and not thinner than number twenty-nine wire gauge, one and five-tenths of one cent per pound ; thinner than number twenty-nine wire gauge, and all iron commercially known as common or black taggers iron, whether put up in boxes or bundles or not, thirty per centum ad valorem.

143. All iron or steel sheets or plates, and all hoop, band, or scroll iron or steel, excepting what are known commercially as tin plates, terne plates, and taggers tin, and hereinafter provided for, when galvanized or coated with zinc or spelter, or other metals, or any alloy of those metals, shall pay three-fourths of one cent per pound more duty than the rates imposed by the preceding paragraph upon the corresponding gauges, or forms, of common or black sheet or taggers iron or steel; and on and after July first, eighteen hundred and ninety one, all iron or steel sheets, or plates, or taggers iron coated with tin or lead or with a mixture of which these metals or either of them is a component part, by the dipping or any other process, and commercially known as tin plates, terne plates, and taggers tin, shall pay two and two-tenths cents per pound : *Provided*, That on and after July first, eighteen hundred and ninety-one, manufactures of which tin, tin plates, terne plates, taggers tin, or either of them, are component materials of chief value, and all articles, vessels or wares manufactured, stamped or drawn from sheet-iron or sheet-steel, such material being the component of chief value, and coated wholly or in part with tin or lead or a mixture of which these metals or either of them is a component part, shall pay a duty of fifty-five per centum ad valorem: *Provided*, That on and after October first, eighteen hundred and ninety-seven, tin plates and terne plates lighter in weight than sixty-three pounds per hundred square feet shall be admitted free of duty, unless it shall be made to appear to the satisfaction of the President (who shall thereupon by proclamation make known the fact) that the aggregate quantity of such plates lighter than sixty-three pounds per hundred square feet produced in the United States during either of the six years next preceding June thirtieth, eighteen hundred and ninety-seven, has equaled one-third the amount of such plates imported and entered for consumption during any fiscal year after the passage of this act, and prior to said October first, eighteen hundred and ninety-seven: *Provided*, That the amount of such plates manufactured into articles exported, and upon which a drawback shall be paid, shall not be included in ascertaining the amount of such importations: *And pro-*

vided further, That the amount or weight of sheet iron or sheet steel manufactured in the United States and applied or wrought in the manufacture of articles or wares tinned or terne-plated in the United States, with weight allowance as sold to manufacturers or others, shall be considered as tin and terne plates produced in the United States within the meaning of this act.

Old law: *And provided,* That on all such iron and steel sheets or plates aforesaid, excepting on what are known commercially as tin-plates, terne-plates, and taggers' tin, and hereafter provided for, when galvanized or coated with zinc or spelter, or other metals, or any alloy of those metals, three-fourths of one cent per pound additional.

Iron or steel sheets, or plates, or taggers iron, coated with tin or lead, or with a mixture of which these metals is a component part, by the dipping or any other process, and commercially known as tin-plates, terne-plates, and taggers tin, one cent per pound; corrugated or crimped sheet-iron or steel, one and four-tenths of one cent per pound.

Manufactures of tin, forty-five per centum.

144. Sheet-iron or sheet-steel, polished, planished, or glanced, by whatever name designated, two and one-half cents per pound : *Provided,* That plate or sheet or taggers iron *or steel,* by whatever name designated, other than the polished, planished, or glanced herein provided for, which has been pickled or cleaned by acid, or by any other material or process, *or* which is cold-rolled, smoothed only, not polished, shall pay one-quarter of one per cent per pound more duty than the corresponding gauges of common or black sheet or taggers iron or steel.

Old law: The words in italics in this paragraph are new matter.

145. Sheets or plates of iron or steel, or taggers iron or steel, coated with tin or lead, or with a mixture of which these metals, or either of them, is a component part, by the dipping or any other process, and commercially known as tin plates, terne plates, and taggers tin, one cent per pound until July first, eighteen hundred and ninety-one.

146. Steel ingots, cogged ingots, blooms, and slabs, by whatever process made ; die blocks or blanks ; billets and bars and tapered or beveled bars ; steamer, crank, and other shafts ; *shafting;* wrist or crank pins ; connecting-rods and piston-rods ; pressed, sheared, or stamped shapes ; saw-plates wholly or partially manufactured ; hammer-molds or swaged steel ; gun-barrel molds not in bars ; alloys used as substitutes for steel tools ; all descriptions and shapes of dry sand, loam, or iron-molded steel castings ; sheets and plates not specially provided for in this act ; and steel in all forms and shapes not specially provided for in this act ; all of the above valued at one cent per pound or less, four-tenths of one cent per pound ; valued above one cent and not above one and four-tenths cents per pound, five-tenths of one cent per pound ; valued above one and four-tenths cents and not above one and eight-tenths cents per pound, eight-tenths of one cent per pound ; valued above one and eight-tenths cents and not above two and two-tenths cents per pound, nine-tenths of one cent per pound ; valued above two and two-tenths cents, and not above three cents per pound, one and two-tenths cents per pound; valued above three cents and not above four cents per pound, one and six-tenths cents per pound ; valued above four cents and not above seven cents per pound, two cents per pound ; valued above seven cents and not above ten cents per pound, two and eight-tenths

cents per pound ; valued above ten cents and not above thirteen cents per pound, three and one-half cents per pound ; valued above thirteen cents and not above sixteen cents per pound, four and two-tenths cents per pound ; valued above sixteen cents per pound, seven cents per pound.

> Old law: Steel ingots, cogged ingots, blooms, and slabs, by whatever process made; die blocks or blanks; billets and bars and tapered or beveled bars; bands, hoops, strips, and sheets of all gauges and widths; plates of all thicknesses and widths; steamer, crank, and other shafts; wrist or crank pins; connecting-rods and piston-rods; pressed, sheared, or stamped shapes, or blanks of sheet or plate steel, or combination of steel and iron, punched or not punched; hammer-molds or swaged steel; gun-molds, not in bars; alloys used as substitutes for steel tools; all descriptions and shapes of dry sand, loam, or iron-molded steel castings, all of the above classes of steel not otherwise specially provided for in this act, valued at four cents a pound or less, forty-five per centum ad valorem; above four cents a pound and not above seven cents per pound, two cents per pound; valued above seven cents and not above ten cents per pound, two and three-fourths cents per pound; valued at above ten cents per pound, three and one-fourth cents per pound:

WIRE—

147. Wire rods : Rivet, screw, fence, and other iron or steel wire rods, and nail rods, whether round, oval, flat, square, or in any other shape, in coils or otherwise, not smaller than number six wire gauge, valued at three and half cents or less per pound, six-tenths of one cent per pound ; and iron or steel, flat, with longitudinal ribs for the manufacture of fencing, valued at three cents or less per pound, six-tenths of one cent per pound : *Provided,* That all iron or steel rods, whether rolled or drawn through dies, smaller than number six wire gauge, shall be classed and dutiable as wire.

> Old law: Iron or steel rivet, screw, nail, and fence, wire rods, round, in coils and loops, not lighter than number five wire gauge, valued at three and one-half cents or less per pound, six-tenths of one cent per pound. Iron or steel, flat, with longitudinal ribs, for the manufacture of fencing, six-tenths of a cent per pound.

148. Wire : Wire made of iron or steel, not smaller than number ten wire gauge, one and one-fourth cents per pound ; smaller than number ten, and not smaller than number sixteen wire gauge, one and three-fourths cents per pound ; smaller than number sixteen and not smaller than number twenty-six wire gauge, two and one-fourth cents per pound ; smaller than number twenty-six wire gauge, three cents per pound : *Provided,* That iron or steel wire covered with cotton, silk, or other material, and wires or strip steel, commonly known as crinoline wire, corset-wire, and hat-wire, shall pay a duty of five cents per pound : *And provided further,* That flat steel wire, or sheet steel in strips, whether drawn through dies or rolls, untempered or tempered, of whatsoever width, twenty-five one thousandths of an inch thick or thinner (ready for use or otherwise), shall pay a duty of fifty per centum ad valorem : *And provided further,* That no article made from iron or steel wire, or of which iron or steel wire is a component part of chief value, shall pay a less rate of duty than the iron or steel wire from which it is made either wholly or in part : *And provided further,* That iron or steel

wire cloths, and iron or steel wire nettings made in meshes of any form, shall pay a duty equal in amount to that imposed on iron or steel wire used in the manufacture of iron or steel wire cloth, or iron or steel wire nettings, and two cents per pound in addition thereto.

Old law: Smaller than number ten gauge, one and one-half and two cents per pound; number ten to number sixteen gauge, two cents; number sixteen to number twenty-six gauge, two and one-half cents; smaller, three cents. *Provided,* That iron or steel wire covered with cotton, silk, or other material, and wire commonly known as crinoline, corset, and hat-wire, shall pay four cents per pound in addition to the foregoing rates: *And provided further,* That no article made from iron or steel wire, or of which iron or steel wire is a component part of chief value, shall pay a less rate of duty than the iron or steel wire from which it is made, either wholly or in part: *And provided further,* That iron or steel wire-cloths, and iron or steel wire-nettings, made in meshes of any form, shall pay a duty equal in amount to that imposed on iron or steel wire of the same gauge, and two cents per pound in addition thereto. There shall be paid on galvanized iron or steel wire (except fence wire) one-half of one cent per pound in addition to the rate imposed on the wire of which it is made. On iron wire-rope and wire-strand, one cent per pound in addition to the rates imposed on the wire of which it is made. On steel wire-rope and wire-strand, two cents per pound in addition to the rates imposed on the wire of which it is made.

There shall be paid on iron or steel wire coated with zinc or tin, or any other metal (except fence-wire and iron or steel, flat, with longitudinal ribs, for the manufacture of fencing), one-half of one cent per pound in addition to the rate imposed on the wire of which it is made; on iron wire rope and wire strand, one cent per pound in addition to the rate imposed on the wire of which it is made; on steel wire rope and wire strand, two cents per pound in addition to the rate imposed on the wire of which they or either of them are made: *Provided further,* That all iron or steel wire valued at more than four cents per pound shall pay a duty of not less than forty-five per centum ad valorem, except that card-wire for the manufacture of card clothing shall pay a duty of thirty-five per centum ad valorem.

GENERAL PROVISIONS.

149. No allowance or reduction of duties for partial loss or damage in consequence of rust or of discoloration shall be made upon any description of iron or steel, or upon any article *wholly or* partly manufactured of iron or steel, or upon any manufacture of iron and steel.

Old law did not contain words in italics.

150. All metal produced from iron or its ores, which is cast and malleable, of whatever description or form, without regard to the percentage of carbon contained therein, whether produced by cementation, or converted, cast, or made from iron or its ores, by the crucible, Bessemer, Clapp-Griffiths, pneumatic, Thomas-Gilchrist, basic, Siemens-Martin, or open-hearth process, or by the equivalent of either, or by a combination of two or more of the processes, or their equivalents, or by any fusion or other process which produces from iron or its ores a metal either granular or fibrous in structure, which

is cast and malleable, excepting what is known as malleable-iron castings, shall be classed and denominated as steel.

151. No article not specially provided for in this act, wholly or partly manufactured from tin plate, terne plate, or the sheet, plate, hoop, band, or scroll iron or steel herein provided for, or of which such tin plate, terne plate, sheet, plate, hoop, band, or scroll iron or steel shall be the material of chief value, shall pay a lower rate of duty than that imposed on the tin plate, terne plate, or sheet, plate, hoop, band, or scroll iron or steel from which it is made, or of which it shall be the component thereof of chief value.

Not in old law.

152. On all iron or steel bars or rods *of whatever shape or section, which are* cold rolled, cold hammered, or polished in any way in addition to the ordinary process of hot rolling or hammering, there shall be paid one-fourth of one cent per pound in addition to the rates provided in this act; *and on all strips, plates, or sheets of iron or steel of whatever shape, other than the polished, planished, or glanced sheet-iron or sheet-steel hereinbefore provided for, which are cold rolled, cold hammered, blued, brightened, tempered, or polished by any process to such perfected surface finish, or polish better than the grade of cold rolled, smooth only, hereinbefore provided for, there shall be paid one and one-fourth cents per pound in addition to the rates provided in this act upon plates, strips, or sheets of iron, or steel of common or black finish;* and on steel circular saw plates there shall be paid one cent per pound in addition to the rate provided in this act for steel saw plates.

Words in italics not in old law.

MANUFACTURES OF IRON AND STEEL.

153. Anchors, or parts thereof, of iron or steel, mill-irons and mill-cranks of wrought-iron, and wrought-iron for ships, and forgings of iron or steel, *or of combined iron and steel,* for vessels, steam-engines, and locomotives, or parts thereof, weighing each twenty-five pounds or more, one and eight-tenths cents per pound.

Old law two cents per pound. Words in italics are new.

154. Axles, or parts thereof, axle-bars, axle-blanks, or forgings for axles, whether of iron or steel, without reference to the stage or state of manufacture, two cents per pound : *Provided, That when iron or steel axles are imported fitted in wheels, or parts of wheels, of iron or steel, they shall be dutiable at the same rate as the wheels in which they are fitted*

Old law; two and a half cents per pound. Proviso in italics is new matter.

155. Anvils of iron or steel, or of iron and steel combined, by whatever process made, or in whatever stage of manufacture, two and one-half cents per pound.

New language. No change in rate.

156. Blacksmiths' hammers and sledges, track tools, wedges, and crowbars, whether of iron or steel, two and one-fourth cents per pound.

Old law: Two and one-half cents per pound.

157. Boiler or other tubes, pipes, flues, or stays of wrought-iron or steel, two and one-half cents per pound.

Old law: Two and one-fourth and three cents per pound.

158. Bolts, with or without threads or nuts, or bolt-blanks, and finished hinges or hinge-blanks, whether of iron or steel, two and one-fourth cents per pound.

Old law: Two and one-half cents per pound.

159. Card-clothing, manufactured from tempered steel wire, fifty cents per square foot; all other, twenty-five cents per square foot.

Old law: Forty-five per centum and twenty-five per centum.

160. Cast-iron pipe of every description, nine-tenths of one cent per pound.

Old law: One cent per pound.

161. Cast-iron vessels, plates, stove-plates, andirons, sad-irons, tailors' irons, hatters' irons, and castings of iron, not specially provided for in this act, one and two-tenths cents per pound.

Old law: One and one-fourth cents per pound.

162. Castings of malleable iron not specially provided for in this act, one and three-fourths cents per pound.

Old law: Two cents per pound.

163. Cast hollow-ware, coated, glazed, or tinned, three cents per pound.

Old law: All hollow-ware, coated, glazed, or tinned, three cents per pound.

164. Chain or chains of all kinds, made of iron or steel, not less than three-fourths of one inch in diameter, one and six-tenths cents per pound; less than three-fourths of one inch and not less than three-eighths of one inch in diameter, one and eight-tenths cents per pound; less than three-eights of one inch in diameter, two and one-half cents per pound, but no chain or chains of any description shall pay a lower rate of duty than forty-five per centum ad valorem.

Old law: One and three-fourths cents per pound; two cents per pound; two and one-half cents per pound.

CUTLERY—

165. Pen-knives or pocket-knives of all kinds, or parts thereof, and erasers, or parts thereof, wholly or partly manufactured, valued at not more than fifty cents per dozen, twelve cents per dozen; valued at more than fifty cents per dozen and not exceeding one dollar and fifty cents per dozen, fifty cents per dozen; valued at more than one dollar and fifty cents per dozen and not exceeding three dollars per dozen, one dollar per dozen; valued at more than three dollars per dozen, two dollars per dozen; and in addition thereto on all the above, fifty per centum ad valorem. Razors and razor-blades, finished or unfinished, valued at less than four dollars per dozen, one dollar per dozen; valued at four dollars or more per dozen, one dollar and seventy-five cents per dozen; and in addition thereto on all the above razors and razor-blades, thirty per centum ad valorem.

Old law: Pen-knives, pocket-knives, of all kinds, and razors, fifty per centum; cutlery not specially provided for, thirty-five per centum.

166. Swords, sword-blades, and side-arms, thirty-five per centum ad valorem.

167. Table-knives, forks, steels, and all butchers', hunting, kitchen, bread, butter, vegetable, fruit, cheese, plumbers', painters', palette, and artists' knives of all sizes, finished or unfinished,

valued at not more than one dollar per dozen pieces, ten cents per dozen; valued at more than one dollar and not more than two dollars, thirty-five cents per dozen; valued at more than two dollars and not more than three dollars, forty cents per dozen; valued at more than three dollars and not more than eight dollars, one dollar per dozen; valued at more than eight dollars, two dollars per dozen; and in addition upon all the above-named articles, thirty per centum ad valorem. All carving and cooks' knives and forks of all sizes, finished or unfinished, valued at not more than four dollars per dozen pieces, one dollar per dozen; valued at more than four dollars and not more than eight dollars, two dollars per dozen pieces; valued at more than eight dollars and not more than twelve dollars, three dollars per dozen pieces; valued at more than twelve dollars, five dollars per dozen pieces; and in addition upon all the above-named articles, thirty per centum ad valorem.

Cutlery not specially provided for, thirty-five per centum.

167. Files, file-blanks, rasps, and floats, of all cuts and kinds, four inches in length and under, thirty-five cents per dozen ; over four inches in length and under nine inches, seventy-five cents per dozen ; nine inches in length and under fourteen inches, one dollar and thirty cents per dozen ; fourteen inches in length and over, two dollars per dozen.

> Old law: Nine inches and under four inches, one dollar and fifty cents per dozen; fourteen inches and over, two dollars and fifty cents per dozen.

FIRE-ARMS—

169. Muskets and sporting rifles, twenty-five per centum ad valorem.

> Old law: Muskets, rifles, and other fire-arms, not specially provided for, twenty-five per centum.

170. All double-barrelled, sporting, breech loading shot-guns valued at not more than six dollars each, one dollar and fifty cents each ; valued at more than six dollars and not more than twelve dollars each, four dollars each ; valued at more than twelve dollars each, six dollars each ; and in addition thereto on all the above, thirty-five per centum ad valorem. Single-barrel breech-loading shot-guns, one dollar each and thirty-five per centum ad valorem. Revolving pistols valued at not more than one dollar and fifty cents each, forty cents each ; valued at more than one dollar and fifty cents, one dollar each ; and in addition thereto on all the above pistols, thirty-five per centum ad valorem.

> Old law: Thirty-five per centum.

171. Iron or steel sheets, plates, wares, or articles, enameled or glazed with vitreous glasses, forty-five per centum ad valorem.

> NOTE.—Not in old law. Rates various.

172. Iron or steel sheets, plates, wares, or articles, enameled or glazed as above with more than one color, or ornamented, fifty per centum ad valorem.

> Not in old law. Rates various.

NAILS, SPIKES, TACKS, AND NEEDLES.

173. Cut nails and cut spikes of iron or steel, one cent per pound.

> Old law: One and one-fourth cents per pound.

174. Horseshoe nails, hob nails, and all other wrought iron or steel nails not specially provided for in this act, four cents per pound.

175. Wire nails made of wrought iron or steel, two inches long and longer, not lighter than number twelve wire gauge, two cents per pound; from one inch to two inches in length, and lighter than number twelve and not lighter than number sixteen wire gauge, two and one-half cents per pound; shorter than one inch and lighter than number sixteen wire gauge, four cents per pound.

> Old law: Four cents per pound.

176. Spikes, nuts, and washers, and horse, mule, or ox shoes, of wrought iron or steel, one and eight-tenths cents per pound.

> Old law: Two cents per pound.

177. Cut tacks, brads, or sprigs, not exceeding sixteen ounces to the thousand, two and one-fourth cents per thousand; exceeding sixteen ounces to the thousand, two and three-fourths cents per pound.

> Old law: Two and one-half cents per pound; three cents per pound.

178. Needles for knitting or sewing machines, crochet-needles and tape-needles and bodkins of metal, thirty-five per centum ad valorem.

> Old law: Twenty-five per centum and thirty-five per centum.

179. Needles, knitting, and all others not specially provided for in this act, twenty-five per centum ad valorem.

PLATES—

180. Steel plates engraved, stereotype plates, *electro-type plates, and plates of other materials, engraved or lithographed, for printing,* twenty-five per centum ad valorem.

> Text in italic is new matter.

181. Railway fish-plates or splice-bars, made of iron or steel, one cent per pound.

> Old law: One and one-fourth cents per pound.

182. Rivets of iron or steel, two and one-half cents per pound.

183. SAWS : Cross-cut saws, eight cents per linear foot; mill, pit, and drag-saws, not over nine inches wide, ten cents per linear foot; over nine inches wide, fifteen cents per linear foot; circular saws, thirty per centum ad valorem; hand, back, and all other saws, not specially provided for in this act, forty per centum ad valorem.

184. Screws, commonly called wood-screws, more than two inches in length, five cents per pound; over one inch and not more than two inches in length, seven cents per pound; over one-half inch and not more than one inch in length, ten cents per pound; one-half inch and less in length, fourteen cents per pound.

> Old law: Six cents per pound; eight cents per pound; ten cents per pound; fourteen cents per pound, respectively.

185. Wheels, or parts thereof, made of iron or steel, and steel-tired wheels for railway purposes, whether wholly or partly finished, and iron or steel locomotive, car, or other railway tires or parts thereof, wholly or partly manufactured, two and one-half cents per pound; and ingots. cogged ingots, blooms, or blanks for the same, without regard to the degree of manufacture, one and three-fourths cents per pound : *Provided,* That when wheels or parts thereof, of iron or steel, are imported with iron or steel axles fitted in them, the

wheels and axles together shall be dutiable at the same rate as is provided for the wheels when imported separately.

Old law: Steel wheels and steel-tired wheels for railway purposes, whether wholly or partly finished, and iron or steel locomotive, car, and other railway tires, or parts thereof, wholly or partly manufactured, two and one half of one cent per pound; iron or steel ingots, cogged ingots, blooms or blanks for the same, without regard to the degree of manufacture, two cents per pound.

MISCELLANEOUS METALS AND MANUFACTURES OF.

186. Aluminium or aluminum, in crude form, and alloys of any kind in which aluminum is the component material of chief value, fifteen cents per pound.

Old law: Free.

187. Antimony, as regulus or metal, three-fourths of one cent per pound.

188. Argentine, albata, or German silver, unmanufactured, twenty-five per centum ad valorem.

189. Brass, in bars or pigs, old brass, clippings from brass or Dutch-metal, *and old sheathing, or yellow metal,* fit only for remanufacture, one and one-half cents per pound.

Words in italic new matter.

190. Bronze powder, twelve cents per pound; bronze or Dutch-metal, or aluminum, in leaf, eight cents per package of one hundred leaves.

Old law: Bronze Dutch metal in leaf, ten per centum; bronze powder, fifteen per centum.

COPPER—

191. Copper imported in the form of ores, one-half of one cent per pound on each pound of fine copper contained therein.

Old law: Two and one-half cents per pound.

192. Old copper, fit only for remanufacture, clippings from new copper, and all composition metal of which copper is a component material of chief value, not specially provided for in this act, one cent per pound.

Old law: Three cents per pound.

193. Regulus of copper and black or coarse copper, and copper cement, one cent per pound on each pound of fine copper contained therein.

Old law: Three and one-half cents per pound.

194. Copper in plates, bars, ingots, Chili or other pigs, and in other forms, not manufactured, not specially provided for in this act, one and one-fourth cents per pound.

Old law: Four cents per pound.

195. Copper in rolled plates, called braziers' copper, sheets, rods, pipes, and copper bottoms, also sheathing or yellow metal of which copper is the component material of chief value, and not composed wholly or in part of iron ungalvanized, thirty-five per centum ad valorem.

In old law, and omitted: Sheathing, or yellow metal, not wholly of copper, nor wholly nor in part of iron, ungalvanized, in sheets, forty-eight inches long and fourteen inches wide, and weighing from fourteen to thirty-four ounces per square foot, thirty-five per centum ad valorem; copper, when imported for the United States Mint, free.

GOLD AND SILVER.—

196. Bullions and metal thread of gold, silver, or other metals, not specially provided for in this act, thirty per centum ad valorem.

> Old law: Twenty-five per centum.

197. Gold-leaf, two dollars per package of five hundred leaves.

> Old law: One dollar and fifty cents per package.

198. Silver-leaf, seventy-five cents per package of five hundred leaves.

> Old law: Seventy-five cents per package.

LEAD.—

199. Lead ore and lead dross, one and one-half cents per pound : *Provided, That silver ore and all other ores containing lead shall pay a duty of one and one-half cents per pound on the lead contained therein, according to sample and assay at the port of entry.*

> Proviso in italics is new matter.

200. Lead in pigs and bars, molten and old refuse lead run into blocks and bars, and old scrap-lead fit only to be remanufactured, two cents per pound.

201. Lead in sheets, pipes, shot, *glaziers' lead, and lead wire,* two and one-half cents per pound.

> Words in italics new matter.
> Old law: Three cents per pound.

202. *Metallic* mineral substances in a crude state and metals unwrought, not specially provided for in this act, twenty per centum ad valorem; mica, thirty-five per centum ad valorem.

> Words in italics new matter; old law: Mica and mica waste free.

NICKEL.—

203. Nickel, nickel oxide, alloy of any kind in which nickel is the component material of chief value, ten cents per pound.

> Old law: Fifteen cents per pound.

204. Pens, metallic, *except gold pens,* twelve cents per gross.

> Words in italics new matter.

205 Pen-holder tips, pen-holders or parts thereof, *and gold pens,* thirty per centum ad valorem.

> Words in italics new matter.

206. Pins, metallic, solid-head or other, *including hair-pins, safetypins, and hat, bonnet, shawl, and bell pins,* thirty per centum ad valorem.

> Words in italics new matter; pins are now classified at various rates.

207. Quicksilver, ten cents per pound. *The flasks, bottles, or other vessels in which quicksilver is imported shall be subject to the same rate of duty as they would be subject to if imported empty.*

> Old law: Ten per centum; part in italics new matter.

208. Type-metal, one and one-half cents per pound *for the lead contained therein;* new types, twenty-five per centum ad valorem.

> Old law: Type metal, twenty per centum; part in italics new matter.

209. Tin : On and after July first, eighteen hundred and ninety-three, there shall be imposed and paid upon cassiterite or black oxide of tin, and upon bar, block, and pig tin, a duty of four cents per

3695——4

pound: *Provided*, That unless it shall be made to appear to the satisfaction of the President of the United States (who shall make known the fact by proclamation) that the product of the mines of the United States shall have exceeded five thousand tons of cassiterite, and bar, block, and pig tin in any one year prior to July first, eighteen hundred and ninety-five, then all imported cassiterite, bar, block, and pig tin shall after July first, eighteen hundred and ninety-five, be admitted free of duty.

Old law: Free.

WATCHES.—

210. Chronometers, box or ship's, and parts thereof, ten per centum ad valorem.

211. Watches, parts of watches, watch-cases, watch movements, *and watch-glasses, whether separately packed or otherwise,* twenty-five per centum ad valorem.

Old law: Watch materials also twenty-five per centum; parts in italics new matter.

ZINC OR SPELTER.—

212. Zinc in blocks or pigs, one and three-fourths cents per pound.

Old law: One and one-half cents per pound.

213. Zinc in sheets, two and one-half cents per pound.

Old law contains the words "spelter or tutenegue."

214. Zinc, old and worn out, fit only to be remanufactured, one and one-fourth cents per pound.

Old law: One and one-half cents per pound.

215. Manufactures, articles, or wares, not specially enumerated or provided for in this act, composed wholly or in part of iron, steel, lead, copper, nickel, pewter, zinc, gold, silver, platinum, *aluminum,* or any other metal, and whether partly or wholly manufactured, forty-five per centum ad valorem.

Words in italics new matter.

Old law: Epaulets, galloons, laces, knots, stars, tassels, and wings of gold, silver or other metal, twenty-five per centum Umbrella and parasol ribs, and stretcher-frames, tips, runners, handles, or other parts thereof, when made in whole or chief parts of iron, steel, or any other metal, forty per centum ad valorem : Britannia ware, and plated and gilt articles and wares of all kinds, thirty-five per centum.

SCHEDULE D.—WOOD AND MANUFACTURES OF.

216. Timber, hewn and sawed, and timber used for spars and in building wharves, ten per centum ad valorem.

Old law: Twenty per centum.

217. Timber, squared or sided, not specially provided for in this act, one-half of one cent per cubic foot.

Old law: One cent per cubic foot.

218. Sawed boards, plank, deals, and other lumber of hemlock, white wood, sycamore, white pine and basswood, one dollar per thousand feet board measure; sawed lumber, not specially provided for in this act, two dollars per thousand feet board measure; but when lumber of any sort is planed or finished, in addition to the rates herein provided, there shall be levied and paid for each side so planed or finished fifty cents per thousand feet board measure; and if planed on one side and tongued and grooved, one dollar per thou-

sand feet board measure; and if planed on two sides, and tongued and grooved, one dollar and fifty cents per thousand feet board measure ; *and in estimating board measure under this schedule no deduction shall be made on board measure on account of planing, tongueing and grooving: Provided, That in case any foreign country shall impose an export duty upon pine, spruce, elm, or other logs, or upon stave bolts, shingle wood, or heading blocks exported to the United States from such country, then the duty upon the sawed lumber herein provided for, when imported from such country, shall remain the same as fixed by the law in force prior to the passage of this act.*

Old law: White pine two dollars per thousand feet; words in italic
new matter.

219. Cedar: That on and after March first, eighteen hundred and ninety-one, paving posts, railroad ties, and telephone and telegraph poles of cedar, shall be dutiable at twenty per centum ad valorem.

Old law: Free.

220. Sawed boards, plank, deals, and all forms of sawed cedar, lignum-vitiae, lancewood, ebony, box, granadilla, mahogany, rosewood, satinwood, and all other cabinet-woods not further manufactured than sawed, fifteen per centum ad valorem; veneers of wood, and wood, unmanufactured, not specially provided for in this act, twenty per centum ad valorem.

Old law: Two dollars per thousand feet; veneers thirty-five per
centum: canes and sticks for walking, if unfinished, twenty
per centum.

221. Pine clapboards, one dollar per one thousand.

Old law: Two dollars per one thousand.

222. Spruce clapboards, one dollar and fifty cents per one thousand.
223. Hubs for wheels, posts, last-blocks, wagon-blocks, oar-blocks, gun-blocks, heading-blocks, and all like blocks or sticks, rough-hewn or sawed only, twenty per centum ad valorem.
224. Laths, fifteen cents per one thousand pieces.
225. Pickets and palings, ten per centum ad valorem.

Old law: Twenty per centum.

226. White pine shingles, twenty cents per one thousand; all other, thirty cents per one thousand.

Old law: Thirty-five cents per one thousand.

227. Staves of wood of all kinds, ten per centum ad valorem.
228. Casks and barrels (empty), sugar-box shooks, and packing-boxes and packing-box shooks, of wood, not specially provided for in this act, thirty per centum ad valorem.
229. Chair cane, or reeds wrought or manufactured from rattans or reeds, and whether round, square, or in any other shape, ten per centum ad valorem.

Old law: Rattans and reeds, manufactured, but not made up into
completed articles, ten per centum ad valorem.

230. House or cabinet furniture, of wood, wholly or partly finished, manufactures of wood, or of which wood is the component material of chief value, not specially provided for in this act, thirty-five per centum ad valorem.

Old law: House or cabinet furniture, in piece[s] or rough, and not
finished, thirty per centum ad valorem.
Cabinet ware[s] and house furniture, finished, thirty-five per
centum ad valorem.

Manufactures of cedar-wood, granadilla, ebony, mahogany, rose wood, and satin wood, thirty-five per centum ad valorem.

Manufactures of wood, or of which wood is the chief component part, not specially enumerated or provided for in this act, thirty-five per centum ad valorem.

Canes and sticks for walking, finished, thirty-five per centum.

Schedule E.—Sugar.

231. That on and after July first, eighteen hundred and ninety-one, and until July first, nineteen hundred and five, there shall be paid, from any moneys in the Treasury not otherwise appropriated, under the provisions of section three thousand six hundred and eighty-nine of the Revised Statutes, to the producer of sugar testing not less than ninety degrees by the polariscope, from beets, sorghum, or sugar-cane grown within the United States, or from maple sap produced within the United States, a bounty of two cents per pound; and upon such sugar testing less than ninety degrees by the polariscope, and not less than eighty degrees, a bounty of one and three-fourth cents per pound, under such rules 'and regulations as the Commissioner of Internal Revenue, with the approval of the Secretary of the Treasury, shall prescribe.

232. The producer of said sugar to be entitled to said bounty shall have first filed prior to July first of each year with the Commissioner of Internal Revenue a notice of the place of production, with a general description of the machinery and methods to be employed by him, with an estimate of the amount of sugar proposed to be produced in the current or next ensuing year, including the number of maple trees to be tapped, and an application for a license to so produce, to be accompanied by a bond in a penalty, and with sureties to be approved by the Commissioner of Internal Revenue, conditioned that he will faithfully observe all rules and regulations that shall be prescribed for such manufacture and production of sugar.

233. The Commissioner of Internal Revenue, upon receiving the application and bond herein before provided for, shall issue to the applicant a license to produce sugar from sorghum, beets, or sugar-cane grown within the United States, or from maple sap produced within the United States at the place and with the machinery and by the methods described in the application ; but said license shall not extend beyond one year from the date thereof.

234. No bounty shall be paid to any person engaged in refining sugars which have been imported into the United States, or produced in the United States upon which the bounty herein provided for has already been paid or applied for, nor to any person unless he shall have first been licensed as herein provided, and only upon sugar produced by such person from sorghum, beets, or sugar-cane grown within the United States, or from maple sap produced within the United States. The Commissioner of Internal Revenue, with the approval of the Secretary of the Treasury, shall from time to time make all needful rules and regulations for the manufacture of sugar from sorghum, beets, or sugar cane grown within the United States, or from maple sap produced within the United States, and shall, under the direction of the Secretary of the Treasury, exercise supervision and inspection of the manufacture thereof.

235. And for the payment of these bounties the Secretary of the Treasury is authorized to draw warrants on the Treasurer of the United

States for such sums as shall be necessary, which sums shall be certified to him by the Commissioner of Internal Revenue, by whom the bounties shall be disbursed, and no bounty shall be allowed or paid to any person licensed as aforesaid in any one year upon any quantity of sugar less than five hundred pounds.

236. That any person who shall knowingly refine or aid in the refining of sugar imported into the United States or upon which the bounty herein provided for has already been paid or applied for, at the place described in the license issued by the Commissioner of Internal Revenue, and any person not entitled to the bounty herein provided for, who shall apply for or receive the same, shall be guilty of a misdemeanor, and, upon conviction thereof, shall pay a fine not exceeding five thousand dollars, or be imprisoned for a period not exceeding five years, or both, in the discretion of the court.

NOTE.—All the foregoing of this schedule is new legislation.

237. All sugars above number sixteen Dutch standard in color shall pay a duty of five-tenths of one cent per pound: *Provided*, That all such sugars above number sixteen Dutch standard in color shall pay one-tenth of one cent per pound in addition to the rate herein provided for, when exported from, or the product of any country when and so long as such country pays, or shall hereafter pay, directly or indirectly, a bounty on the exportation of any sugar that may be included in this grade which is greater than is paid on raw sugars of a lower saccharine strength; and the Secretary of the Treasury shall prescribe suitable rules and regulations to carry this provision into effect: *And provided further*, That all machinery purchased abroad and erected in a beet-sugar factory and used in the production of raw sugar in the United States from beets produced therein shall be admitted duty free until the first day of July, eighteen hundred and ninety-two: *Provided*, That any duty collected on any of the above-described machinery purchased abroad and imported into the United States for the uses above indicated since January first, eighteen hundred and ninety, shall be refunded.

Old law: Sixteen to twenty Dutch standard, three cents per pound; above twenty, three and fifty one hundredths cents per pound.
Beet sugar machinery dutiable at forty-five per centum. *

238. Sugar candy and all confectionery, including chocolate confectionery, made wholly or in part of sugar, valued at twelve cents or less per pound, and on sugars after being refined, when tinctured, colored, or in any way adulterated, five cents per pound.

239. All other confectionery, including chocolate confectionery, not specially provided for in this act, fifty per centum ad valorem.

Old law for paragraphs 238 and 239: Sugar candy, not colored, five cents per pound.
All other confectionery, not specially enumerated or provided for in this act, made wholly or in part of sugar, and on sugars after being refined, when tinctured, colored, or in any way adulterated, valued at thirty cents per pound or less, ten cents per pound.
Confectionery valued above thirty cents per pound, or when sold by the box, package, or otherwise than by the pound, fifty per centum ad valorem.

240. Glucose or grape sugar, three-fourths of one cent per pound.

Old law: Glucose, twenty per centum.

241. That the provisions of this act providing terms for the admission of imported sugars and molasses and for the payment of

* See Free List for sugar not above No. 13, D. S.

a bounty on sugars of domestic production shall take effect on the first day of April, eighteen hundred and ninety-one: *Provided*, That on and after the first day of March, eighteen hundred and ninety-one, and prior to the first day of April, eighteen hundred and ninety-one, sugars not exceeding number sixteen Dutch standard in color may be refined in bond without payment of duty, and such refined sugars may be transported in bond and stored in bonded warehouse at such points of destination as are provided in existing laws relating to the immediate transportation of dutiable goods in bond, under such rules and regulations as shall be prescribed by the Secretary of the Treasury.

Note.—All new matter.

SCHEDULE F.—TOBACCO AND MANUFACTURES OF.

242. Leaf tobacco suitable for cigar-wrappers, if not stemmed, two dollars per pound ; if stemmed, two dollars and seventy-five cents per pound : *Provided*, That if any portion of any tobacco imported in any bale, box, or package, or in bulk shall be suitable for cigar-wrappers, the entire quantity of tobacco contained in such bale, box, or package, or bulk shall be dutiable ; if not stemmed, at two dollars per pound ; if stemmed, at two dollars and seventy-five cents per pound.

> Old law: Leaf tobacco, of which eighty-five per centum is of the requisite size and of the necessary fineness of texture to be suitable for wrappers, and of which more than one hundred leaves are required to weigh a pound, if not stemmed, seventy-five cents per pound ; if stemmed, one dollar per pound.

243. All other tobacco in leaf, unmanufactured and not stemmed, thirty-five cents per pound ; if stemmed, fifty cents per pound.

> Old law: Stemmed, forty cents per pound.

244. Tobacco, manufactured, of all descriptions, not specially enumerated or provided for in this act, forty cents per pound.

245. Snuff and snuff flour, manufactured of tobacco, ground dry, or damp, and pickled, scented, or otherwise, of all descriptions, fifty cents per pound.

246. Cigars, cigarettes, and cheroots of all kinds, four dollars and fifty cents per pound and twenty-five per centum ad valorem; and paper cigars and cigarettes, including wrappers, shall be subject to the same duties as are herein imposed upon cigars.

> Old law: Two dollars and fifty cents per pound and twenty-five per centum.

SCHEDULE G.—AGRICULTURAL PRODUCTS AND PROVISIONS.

ANIMALS, LIVE—
247. Horses and mules, thirty dollars per head: *Provided*, That horses valued at one hundred and fifty dollars and over shall pay a duty of thirty per centum ad valorem.
248. Cattle, more than one year old, ten dollars per head ; one year old or less, two dollars per head.
249. Hogs, one dollar and fifty cents per head.
250. Sheep, one year old or more, one dollar and fifty cents per head ; less than one year old, seventy-five cents per head.

251. All other live animals, not specially provided for in this act, twenty per centum ad valorem.

> Old law, covering paragraphs 235 to 239: Animals, live, twenty per centum.

BREADSTUFFS AND FARINACEOUS SUBSTANCES—

252. Barley, thirty cents per bushel of forty-eight pounds.

> Old law: Ten cents per bushel.

253. Barley-malt, forty-five cents per bushel of thirty-four pounds.

> Old law: Twenty cents per bushel.

254. Barley, pearled, patent, or hulled, two cents per pound.

> Old law: One-half cent per pound.

255. Buckwheat, fifteen cents per bushel of forty-eight pounds.

> Old law: Unenumerated, ten per centum.

256. Corn or maize, fifteen cents per bushel of fifty-six pounds.

> Old law: Ten cents per bushel.

257. Corn-meal, twenty cents per bushel of forty-eight pounds.

> Old law: Ten cents per bushel.

258. Macaroni, vermicelli, and all similar preparations, two cents per pound.

> Old law: Free.

259. Oats, fifteen cents per bushel.

> Old law: Ten cents per bushel.

260. Oatmeal, one cent per pound.

> Old law: One-half cent per pound.

261. Rice, cleaned, two cents per pound; uncleaned rice, one and one-quarter cents per pound; paddy, three-quarters of one cent per pound; rice-flour, rice-meal, and rice, broken, which will pass through a sieve known commercially as number twelve wire sieve, one-fourth of one cent per pound.

> Old law: Cleaned, two and one-quarter cents per pound; uncleaned, one and one-half cents per pound; paddy, one and one-quarter cents per pound; rice flour, rice meal, twenty per centum.

262. Rye, ten cents per bushel.

263. Rye-flour, one-half of one cent per pound.

264. Wheat, twenty-five cents per bushel.

> Old law: Twenty cents per bushel.

265. Wheat-flour, twenty-five per centum ad valorem.

> Old law: Twenty per centum.

DAIRY PRODUCTS—

266. Butter, and substitutes therefor, six cents per pound.

> Old law: Four cents per pound.

267. Cheese, six cents per pound.

> Old law: Four cents per pound.

268. Milk, fresh, five cents per gallon.

> Old law: Ten per centum (unenumerated).

269. Milk, preserved or condensed, including weight of packages, three cents per pound; sugar of milk, eight cents per pound.

> Old law: Milk, condensed, twenty per centum; milk, sugar of, free.

FARM AND FIELD PRODUCTS—

270. Beans, forty cents per bushel of sixty pounds

> Old law: Unenumerated, ten per centum.

271. Beans, pease, and mushrooms, prepared or preserved, in tins, jars, bottles, or otherwise, forty per centum ad valorem.
   Old law: Vegetables, prepared or preserved, of all kinds not otherwise provided for, thirty per centum.

272. Broom-corn, eight dollars per ton.
   Old law: Ten per centum (unenumerated).

273. Cabbages, three cents each.
   Old law: Ten per centum (unenumerated).

274. Cider, five cents per gallon.
   Old law: Twenty per centum (unenumerated).

275. Eggs, five cents per dozen.
   Old law: Free.

276. Eggs, yolk of, twenty-five per centum ad valorem.
   Old law: Unenumerated, twenty per centum.

277. Hay, four dollars per ton.
   Old law: Two dollars per ton.

278. Honey, twenty cents per gallon.

279. Hops, fifteen cents per pound.
   Old law: Eight cents per pound.

280. Onions, forty cents per bushel.
   Old law: Ten per centum (unenumerated).

281. Pease, green, in bulk or in barrels, sacks, or similar packages, forty cents per bushel of sixty pounds; pease, dried, twenty cents per bushel; split pease, fifty cents per bushel of sixty pounds: pease in cartons, papers, or other small packages, one cent per pound.
   Old law: Vegetables in natural state, ten per centum; split pease, twenty per centum; for seed, twenty per centum.

282. Plants, trees, shrubs, and vines of all kinds, commonly known as nursery stock, not specially provided for in this act, twenty per centum ad valorem.
   Old law: Plants, trees, shrubs, and vines of all kinds not otherwise provided for, and seeds of all kinds, except medicinal seeds not specially enumerated or provided for in this act, free.

283. Potatoes, twenty-five cents per bushel of sixty pounds.
   Old law: Fifteen cents per bushel.

SEEDS—

284. Castor beans or seeds, fifty cents per bushel of fifty pounds.

285. Flaxseed or linseed, *poppy seed and other oil seeds, not specially provided for in this act,* thirty cents per bushel of fifty-six pounds; but no drawback shall be allowed on oil-cake made from imported seed.
   Old law: Twenty cents per bushel.

286. Garden-seeds, agricultural seeds, and other seeds, not specially provided for in this act, twenty per centum ad valorem
   Old law: Garden seeds, twenty per centum, and most other seeds free.

287. Vegetables of all kinds, prepared or preserved, including pickles and sauces of all kinds, not specially provided for in this act, forty-five per centum ad valorem.
   Old law: Vegetables of all kinds, thirty per centum; pickles and sauces, and so forth, thirty-five per centum; vegetables in salt or brine, ten per centum.

288. Vegetables in their natural state, not specially provided for in this act, twenty-five per centum ad valorem.

> Old law: Vegetables in their natural state or in salt or brine, ten per centum.

289. Straw, thirty per centum ad valorem.

> Old law: Unmanufactured, free.

290. Teazles, thirty per centum ad valorem.

> Old law: Free.

FISH—

291. Anchovies and sardines, packed in oil or otherwise, in tin boxes measuring not more than five inches long, four inches wide and three and one-half inches deep, ten cents per whole box; in half-boxes, measuring not more than five inches long, four inches wide, and one and five-eighths inches deep, five cents each; in quarter-boxes, measuring not more than four and three-fourths inches long, three and one-half inches wide, and one and one-fourth inches deep, two and one-half cents each; when imported in any other form, forty per centum ad valorem.

292. Fish, pickled, in barrels or half barrels, and mackerel or salmon, pickled or salted, one cent per pound.

> Old law: Mackerel, one cent per pound; salmon, pickled, one cent per pound; other fish, pickled or salted, one cent per pound.

293. Fish, smoked, dried, salted, pickled, frozen, packed in ice, or otherwise prepared for preservation, and fresh fish, not specially provided for in this act, three-fourths of one cent per pound.

> Old law: Foreign-caught fish, imported otherwise than in barrels or half barrels, whether fresh, smoked, dried, salted, or pickled, not specially enumerated or provided for in this act, fifty cents per hundred pounds.

294. Herrings, pickled or salted, one-half of one cent per pound; herrings, fresh, one-fourth of one cent per pound.

> Old law: Herrings, fresh, fifty cents per hundred pounds.

295. Fish in cans or packages made of tin or other material, except anchovies and sardines and fish packed in any other manner, not specially enumerated or provided for in this act, thirty per centum ad valorem.

> Old law: Fish preserved in oil, except anchovies and sardines, thirty per centum.
> Old law: Salmon and all other fish prepared or preserved not otherwise provided for, twenty-five per centum.

296. Cans or packages, made of tin or other metal, containing shell fish admitted free of duty, not exceeding one quart in contents, shall be subject to a duty of eight cents per dozen cans or packages ; and when exceeding one quart, shall be subject to an additional duty of four cents per dozen for each additional half quart or fractional part thereof; *Provided*, That until June thirtieth, eighteen hundred and ninety-one, such cans or packages shall be admitted as now provided by law.

> Old law: Cans or packages made of tin or other material containing fish of any kind admitted free of duty under any existing law or treaty, not exceeding one quart in contents, shall be subject to a duty of one cent and a half on each can or package: and when exceeding one quart, shall be subject to an additional duty of one cent and a half for each additional quart or fractional part thereof.

FRUITS AND NUTS—

Fruits:

297. Apples, green or ripe, twenty-five cents ᵖⁱ ... ʳ ⁱshel.
Old law: Free, unenumerated.

298. Apples, dried, dessiccated, evaporated, or prepared in any manner, and not otherwise provided for in this act, two cents per pound.
Old law: Thirty-five per centum or free, unenumerated.

299. Grapes, sixty cents per barrel of three cubic feet capacity or fractional part thereof; plums, and prunes, two cents per pound.
Old law: Preserved prunes, one cent per pound; grapes, twenty per centum.

300. Figs, two and one-half cents per pound.
Old law: Two cents per pound.

301. Oranges, lemons, and limes, in packages of capacity of one and one-fourth cubic feet or less, thirteen cents per package; in packages of capacity exceeding one and one-fourth cubic feet and not exceeding two and one-half cubic feet, twenty-five cents per package; in packages of capacity exceeding two and one-half cubic feet and not exceeding five cubic feet, fifty cents per package; in packages of capacity exceeding five cubic feet, for every additional cubic foot or fractional part thereof, ten cents; in bulk, one dollar and fifty cents per one thousand; and in addition thereto a duty of thirty per centum ad valorem upon the boxes or barrels containing such oranges, lemons, or limes.
Old law: Oranges, in boxes of capacity not exceeding two and one-half cubic feet, twenty-five cents per box; in one-half boxes, capacity not exceeding one and one-fourth cubic feet, thirteen cents per half box; in bulk, one dollar and sixty cents per thousand; in barrels, capacity not exceeding that of the one hundred and ninety-six pounds flour barrel, fifty-five cents per barrel.
Lemons, in boxes of capacity not exceeding two and one-half cubic feet, thirty cents per box; in one-half boxes, capacity not exceeding one and one-fourth cubic feet, sixteen cents per half box; in bulk, two dollars per thousand.
Lemons and oranges, in packages, not specially enumerated or provided for in this act, twenty per centum ad valorem.
Limes, twenty per centum ad valorem.

302. Raisins, two and one-half cents per pound.
Old law: Two cents per pound.

303. Comfits, sweetmeats, and fruits preserved in sugar, sirup, molasses, or spirits not specially provided for in this act, and jellies of all kinds, thirty-five per centum ad valorem.

304. Fruits preserved in their own juices, thirty per centum ad valorem.
Old law: Twenty per centum.

305. Orange-peel and lemon-peel, preserved or candied, two cents per pound.
Old law: Thirty-five per centum.

Nuts:

306. Almonds, not shelled, five cents per pound; clear almonds, shelled, seven and one-half cents per pound.

307. Filberts and walnuts of all kinds, not shelled, three cents per pound; shelled, six cents per pound.

> Old law: Shelled, three cents per pound.

308. Peanuts or ground beans, unshelled, one cent per pound; shelled, one and one-half cents per pound.

> Old law: Shelled, one cent per pound.

309. Nuts of all kinds, shelled or unshelled, not specially provided for in this act, one and one-half cents per pound.

> Old law: Two cents per pound.

MEAT PRODUCTS—

310. Bacon and hams, five cents per pound.

> Old law: Two cents per pound.

311. Beef, *mutton*, and pork, two cents per pound.

> Old law: One cent per pound; mutton (unenumerated), ten per centum.

312. Meats of all kinds, prepared or preserved, not specially provided for in this act, twenty-five per centum ad valorem.

> Old law: Prepared meats of all kinds, not specially provided for, twenty-five per centum.

313. Extract of meat, all not specially provided for in this act, thirty-five cents per pound ; fluid extract of meat, fifteen cents per pound ; and no separate or additional duty shall be collected on such coverings unless as such they are suitable and apparently designed for use other than in the importation of meat extracts.

> Old law, text: Extract of meat, twenty per centum.

314. Lard, two cents per pound.

315. Poultry, live, three cents per pound; dressed, five cents per pound.

> Old law: Poultry, dressed (unenumerated), ten per centum.

316. Tallow, one cent per pound; *wool grease, including that known commercially as degras or brown wool grease, one-half of one cent per pound.*

> Old law : Degras (unenumerated), ten per centum. New matter in italics.

MISCELLANEOUS PRODUCTS—

317. Chicory-root, burnt or roasted, ground or granulated, or in rolls, or otherwise prepared, and not specially provided for in this act, two cents per pound.

> Old law: Chickory-root, ground or unground, burnt or prepared, two cents per pound. Change of text.

318. Chocolate, (*other than chocolate confectionery and chocolate commercially known as sweetened chocolate,*) two cents per pound.

> NOTE.—Words in italics new matter.

319. Cocoa, prepared or manufactured, not specially provided for in this act, two cents per pound.

320. Cocoa-butter or cocoa-butterine, three and one-half cents per pound.

> Old law: Not enumerated, twenty-five per centum.

321. Dandelion-root and acorns prepared, and other articles used as coffee, or as substitutes for coffee, not specially provided for in this act, one and one-half cents per pound.

> Old law: Acorns, and dandelion root, raw or prepared, and all other articles used or intended to be used as coffee, or as substitutes therefor, not specially enumerated or provided for in this act, two cents per pound.

SALT.

322. Salt in bags, sacks, barrels, or other packages twelve cents per one hundred pounds; in bulk, eight cents per one hundred pounds: *Provided,* That imported salt in bond may be used in curing fish taken by vessels licensed to engage in the fisheries, and in curing fish on the shores of the navigable waters of the United States, under such regulations as the Secretary of the Treasury shall prescribe; and upon proof that the salt has been used for either of the purposes stated in this proviso, the duties on the same shall be remitted: *Provided further,* That exporters of meats, whether packed or smoked, which have been cured in the United States with imported salt, shall, upon satisfactory proof, under such regulations as the Secretary of the Treasury shall prescribe, that such meats have been cured with imported salt, have refunded to them from the Treasury the duties paid on the salt so used in curing such exported meats, in amounts not less than one hundred dollars.

323. Starch, including all preparations, from whatever substance produced, fit for use as starch, two cents per pound

> Old law: Potato or corn starch, two cents per pound; rice starch, two and a half cents per pound: other starch, two and a half cents per pound. Root flour free.

324. Dextrine, burnt starch, gum substitute, or British gum, one and one-half cents per pound.

> Old law : One cent per pound.

325. Mustard, ground or preserved, in bottles or otherwise, ten cents per pound.

326. Spices, ground or powdered, not specially provided for in this act, four cents per pound ; cayenne pepper, two and one-half cents per pound, unground ; sage, three cents per pound.

> Old law: Spices five cents per pound
> Old law: Sage not enumerated but free by Treasury ruling when unground.

327. Vinegar, seven and one-half cents per gallon. The standard for Vinegar shall be taken to be that strength which requires thirty-five grains of bicarbonate of potash to neutralize one ounce troy of vinegar.

> Omitted from new law, "and all import duties that may by law be imposed on vinegar imported from foreign countries shall be collected according to this standard."

328. There shall be allowed on the imported tin-plate used in the manufacture of cans, boxes, packages, and all articles of tin ware exported, either empty or filled with domestic products, a drawback equal to the duty paid on such tin-plate, less one per centum of such duty, which shall be retained for the use of the United States.

> New matter.

Schedule H.—Spirits, Wines, and Other Beverages.

Spirits.—

329. Brandy and other spirits manufactured or distilled from grain or other materials, and not specially provided for in this act, two dollars and fifty cents per proof gallon.

    Old law: Two dollars per gallon.

330. Each and every gauge or wine gallon of measurement shall be counted as at least one proof gallon ; and the standard for determining the proof of brandy and other spirits or liquors of any kind imported shall be the same as that which is defined in the laws relating to internal revenue ; but any brandy or other spirituous liquors, imported in casks of less capacity than fourteen gallons, shall be forfeited to the United States : *Provided, That it shall be lawful for the Secretary of the Treasury, in his discretion, to authorize the ascertainment of the proof of wines, cordials, or other liquors, by distillation or otherwise, in case where it is impracticable to ascertain such proof by the means prescribed by existing law or regulations.*

    Note.—New matter in italics.

331. On all compounds or preparations of which distilled spirits are a component part of chief value, not specially provided for in this act, there shall be levied a duty not less than that imposed upon distilled spirits.

332. Cordials, liquors, arrack, absinthe, kirschwasser, ratafia, and other spirituous beverages or bitters *of all kinds* containing spirits, and not specially provided for in this act, two dollars and fifty cents per proof gallon.

    Old law: Two dollars per gallon. New matter in italics.

333. No lower rate or amount of duty shall be levied, collected, and paid on brandy, spirits, and other spirituous beverages than that fixed by law for the description of first proof; but it shall be increased in proportion for any greater strength than the strength of first proof, and all imitations of brandy or spirits or wines imported by any names whatever shall be subject to the highest rate of duty provided for the genuine articles respectively intended to be represented, and in no case less than one dollar and fifty cents per gallon.

    Old law: One dollar per gallon.
    Old law: Distilled spirits, containing fifty per centum of anhydrous alcohol, one dollar per gallon.
    Alcohol, containing ninety-four per cent. anhydrous alcohol, two dollars per gallon.

334. Bay-rum or bay-water, whether distilled or compounded, of first proof, and in proportion for any greater strength than first proof, one dollar and fifty cents per gallon.

    Old law: One dollar per gallon.

Wines :

335. Champagne and all other sparkling wines, in bottles containing each not more than one quart and more than one pint, eight dollars per dozen ; containing not more than one pint each and more than one-half pint, four dollars per dozen; containing one-half pint each or less, two dollars per dozen; in bottles *or other vessels* containing more than one quart

each, in addition to eight dollars per dozen bottles, on the quantity in excess of one quart, at the rate of two dollars and fifty cents per gallon.

Old law: Seven dollars, three dollars and fifty cents, and one dollar and seventy-five cents in bottles, and two dollars and twenty-five cents per gallon ; new matter in italics.

336. Still wines, *including ginger wine or ginger cordial* and vermuth, in casks, fifty cents per gallon; in bottles or jugs, per case of one dozen bottles or jugs, containing each not more than one quart and more than one pint, or twenty-four bottles or jugs containing each not more than one pint, one dollar and sixty cents per case; and any excess beyond these quantities found in such bottles or jugs shall be subject to a duty of five cents per pint or fractional part thereof, but no separate or additional duty shall be assessed on the bottles or jugs: *Provided, That any wines, ginger-cordial, or vermuth imported containing more than twenty-four per centum of alcohol shall be forfeited to the United States: And provided further, That there shall be no constructive or other allowance for breakage, leakage, or damage on wines,* liquors, cordials, or distilled spirits. Wines, *cordials,* brandy, and other spirituous liquors imported in bottles *or jugs* shall be packed in packages containing not less than one dozen bottles *or jugs* in each package; and all such bottles *or jugs* shall pay an additional duty of three cents for each bottle *or jug unless specially provided for in this act.*

Old law. New matter in italics.

337. Ale, porter, and beer, in bottles or jugs, forty cents per gallon, but no separate or additional duty shall be assessed on the bottles or jugs; otherwise than in bottles or jugs, twenty cents per gallon.

Old law: Thirty-five cents per gallon: twenty cents per gallon.
NOTE.—The words of limitation, "glass, stone, or earthenware," omitted from new law.

338. Malt extract, fluid, in casks, twenty cents per gallon; in bottles or jugs, forty cents per gallon; solid or condensed, forty per centum ad valorem.

Old law: Same as ale, beer, and porter, unless proprietary, which was fifty per centum.

339. Cherry juice and prune juice, or prune wine, and other fruit juice, not specially provided for in this act, containing not more than eighteen per centum of alcohol, sixty cents per gallon: if containing more than eighteen per centum of alcohol, two dollars and fifty cents per proof gallon.

Old law: Cherry juice, twenty per centum; prune juice, unenumerated, twenty per centum.

340. Ginger-ale, ginger-beer, lemonade, soda-water, and other similar waters in plain green, or colored, molded or pressed glass bottles, containing each not more than three-fourths of a pint thirteen cents per dozen ; containing more than three-fourths of a pint each and not more than one and one-half pints, twenty-six cents per dozen ; but no separate or additional duty shall be assessed on the bottles ; if imported otherwise than in plain green or colored molded or pressed

glass bottles, or in such bottles containing more than one and one-half pints each, fifty cents per gallon and in addition thereto, duty shall be collected on the bottles, or other coverings, at the rates which would be chargeable thereon if imported empty.

Old law: Ginger ale or ginger beer, twenty per centum ad valorem, but no separate or additional duty shall be collected on bottles or jugs containing the same.

341. All mineral waters, and all imitations of natural mineral waters, and all artificial mineral waters not specially provided for in this act, in plain or colored glass bottles, containing not more than one pint, sixteen cents per dozen bottles. If containing more than one pint and not more than one quart, twenty-five cents per dozen bottles. But no separate duty shall be assessed upon the bottles. If imported otherwise than in plain green or colored glass bottles, or if imported in such bottles containing more than one quart, twenty cents per gallon, and in addition thereto duty shall be collected upon the bottles or other covering at the same rates that would be charged if imported empty or separately.

Old law: All imitations of natural mineral waters and all artificial mineral waters, thirty per centum ad valorem.

SCHEDULE I.—COTTON MANUFACTURERS.

342. Cotton thread, yarn, warps, or warp-yarn, whether single or advanced beyond the condition of single, by grouping or twisting two or more single yarns together, whether on beams or in bundles, skeins, or cops, or in any other form, *except spool-thread of cotton, hereinafter provided for*, valued at not exceeding twenty-five cents per pound, ten cents per pound ; valued at over twenty-five cents per pound and not exceeding forty cents per pound, eighteen cents per pound ; valued at over forty cents per pound and not exceeding fifty cents per pound, twenty-three cents per pound ; valued at over fifty cents per pound and not exceeding sixty cents per pound, twenty-eight cents per pound ; valued at over sixty cents per pound and not exceeding seventy cents per pound, thirty-three cents per pound ; valued at over seventy cents per pound and not exceeding eighty cents per pound, thirty-eight cents per pound ; valued at over eighty cents per pound and not exceeding one dollar per pound, forty-eight cents per pound ; valued at over one dollar per pound, fifty per centum ad valorem.

Old law: Valued at twenty-five to forty cents, eighteen cents per pound; valued at forty to fifty cents, twenty cents per pound; valued at fifty to sixty cents, twenty-five cents per pound.

NOTE.—New matter in italics,

343. Spool-thread of cotton, containing on each spool not exceeding one hundred yards of thread, seven cents per dozen ; exceeding one hundred yards on each spool, for every additional one hundred yards of thread or fractional part thereof in excess of one hundred yards, seven cents per dozen spools.

344. Cotton cloth not bleached, dyed, colored, stained, painted, or printed, and not exceeding fifty threads to the square inch, counting the warp and filling, two cents per square yard ; if bleached, two

and one-half cents per square yard ; if dyed, colored, stained, painted, or printed, four cents per square yard.

Old law: Two and one-half cents per square yard; three and one-half cents per square yard; four and one-half cents per square yard.

345. Cotton cloth, not bleached, dyed, colored, stained, painted, or printed, exceeding fifty and not exceeding one hundred threads to the square inch, counting the warp and filling, two and one-fourth cents per square yard ; if bleached, three cents per square yard ; if dyed, colored, stained, painted, or printed, four cents per square yard : *Provided, That on all cotton cloth not exceeding one hundred threads to the square inch, counting the warp and filling, not bleached, dyed, colored, stained, painted, or printed, valued at over six and one-half cents per square yard; bleached, valued at over nine cents per square yard; and dyed, colored, stained, painted, or printed, valued at over twelve cents per square yard, there shall be levied, collected, and paid a duty of thirty-five per centum ad valorem.*

Old law: Two and one-half cents per square yard; three and one-half cents per square yard; four and one-half cents per square yard.
NOTE.—New matter in italics.

346. Cotton cloth, not bleached, dyed, colored, stained, painted, or printed, exceeding one hundred and not exceeding one hundred and fifty threads to the square inch, counting the warp and filling, three cents per square yard ; if bleached, four cents per square yard ; if dyed, colored, stained, painted, or printed, five cents per square yard : *Provided,* That on all cotton cloth exceeding one hundred and not exceeding one hundred and fifty threads to the square inch, counting the warp and filling, not bleached, dyed, colored, stained, painted, or printed, valued at over seven and one-half cents per square yard ; bleached, valued at over ten cents per square yard ; dyed, colored, stained, painted, or printed, valued at over twelve and one-half cents per square yard, there shall be levied, collected, and paid a duty of forty per centum ad valorem.

Old law: Three cents per square yard, four cents per square yard, five cents per square yard; if valued above eight cents, ten cents, and thirteen cents per square yard, respectively, to pay forty per centum.

347. Cotton cloth, not bleached, dyed, colored, stained, painted, or printed, exceeding one hundred and fifty and not exceeding two hundred threads to the square inch, counting the warp and filling, three and a half cents per square yard; if bleached, four and one-half cents per square yard; if dyed, colored, stained, painted, or printed, five and one-half cents per square yard: *Provided,* That on all cotton cloth exceeding one hundred and fifty and not exceeding two hundred threads to the square inch, counting the warp and filling, not bleached, dyed, colored, stained, painted, or printed, valued at over eight cents per square yard; bleached valued at over ten cents per square yard; dyed, colored, stained, painted, or printed, valued at over twelve cents per square yard, there shall be levied, collected, and paid a duty of forty-five per centum ad valorem.

Old law: Three cents per square yard, four cents per square yard five cents per square yard: if valued above eight cents, ten cents and thirteen cents per square yard, respectively, to pay forty per centum.

348. Cotton cloth, not bleached, dyed, colored, stained, painted, or printed, exceeding two hundred threads to the square inch, counting

the warp and filling, four and one-half cents per square yard; if bleached, five and one-half cents per square yard; if dyed, colored, stained, painted, or printed, six and three-fourths cents per square yard: *Provided*, That on all such cotton cloths not bleached, dyed, colored, stained, painted, or printed, valued at over ten cents per square yard; bleached, valued at over twelve cents per square yard; and dyed, colored, stained, painted, or printed, valued at over fifteen cents per square yard, there shall be levied, collected, and paid a duty of forty-five per centum ad valorem: *Provided further, That on cotton cloth, bleached, dyed, colored, stained, painted or printed, containing an admixture of silk, and not otherwise provided for, there shall be levied, collected, and paid a duty of ten cents per square yard, and in addition thereto thirty-five per centum ad valorem.*

Old law: Four cents per square yard, five cents per square yard, six cents per square yard; if valued above ten cents, twelve cents and fifteen cents per square yard, respectively, to pay forty per centum.

NOTE.—New matter in italics.

349. Clothing ready made, and articles of wearing apparel of every description, handkerchiefs, and neckties or neck wear composed of cotton or other vegetable fiber, or of which cotton or other vegetable fiber is the component material of chief value, made up or manufactured wholly or in part by the tailor, seamstress, or manufacturer, all of the foregoing not specially provided for in this act, fifty per centum ad valorem: *Provided*, That all such clothing ready made and articles of wearing apparel having India rubber as a component material (not including gloves or elastic articles that are specially provided for in this act), shall be subject to a duty of fifty cents per pound, and in addition thereto fifty per centum ad valorem.

Old law: Corsets, thirty-five per centum, of whatever material composed; handkerchiefs, forty per centum; other items, thirty-five per centum; hat bodies of cotton, thirty-five per centum.

350. Plushes, velvets, velveteens, corduroys, and all pile fabrics composed of cotton or other vegetable fiber, not bleached, dyed, colored, stained, painted, or printed, ten cents per square yard and twenty per centum ad valorem; on all such goods if bleached, twelve cents per square yard and twenty per centum ad valorem; if dyed, colored, stained, painted, or printed, fourteen cents per square yard and twenty per centum ad valorem; but none of the foregoing articles in this paragraph shall pay a less rate of duty than forty per centum ad valorem.

Old law: Cotton velvet, forty per centum; corduroys, thirty-five per centum; plush, thirty-five per centum.

351. Chenille curtains, table covers, and all goods manufactured of cotton chenille, or of which cotton chenille forms the component material of chief value, sixty per centum ad valorem.

New provision: Treasury ruling forty per centum.

352. Stockings, hose and half-hose, made on knitting machines or frames, composed of cotton or other vegetable fiber and not otherwise specially provided for in this act, and shirts and drawers composed of cotton, valued at not more than one dollar and fifty cents per dozen, thirty-five per centum ad valorem.

Old law: On stockings, hose, half-hose, shirts, and drawers, and all goods made on knitting machines or frames, composed wholly of cotton, and not herein otherwise provided for, thirty-five per centum ad valorem.

353. Stockings, hose, and half-hose, selvedged, fashioned, narrowed, or shaped wholly or in part by knitting-machines or frames, or knit by hand, including such as are commercially known as seamless stockings, hose or half-hose, all of the above composed of cotton or other vegetable fiber, finished or unfinished, valued at not more than sixty cents per dozen pairs, twenty cents per dozen pairs, and in addition thereto twenty per centum ad valorem; valued at more than sixty cents per dozen pairs and not more than two dollars per dozen pairs, fifty cents per dozen pairs, and in addition thereto thirty per centum ad valorem; valued at more than two dollars per dozen pairs, and not more than four dollars per dozen pairs, seventy-five cents per dozen pairs, and in addition thereto, forty per centum ad valorem; valued at more than four dollars per dozen pairs, one dollar per dozen pairs, and in addition thereto, forty per centum ad valorem; and all shirts and drawers composed of cotton or other vegetable fiber, valued at more than one dollar and fifty cents per dozen and not more than three dollars per dozen, one dollar per dozen, and in addition thereto, thirty-five per centum ad valorem; valued at more than three dollars per dozen, and not more than five dollars per dozen, one dollar and twenty-five cents per dozen, and in addition thereto, forty per centum ad valorem; valued at more than five dollars per dozen, and not more than seven dollars per dozen, one dollar and fifty cents per dozen, and in addition thereto, forty per centum ad valorem; valued at more than seven dollars per dozen, two dollars per dozen, and in addition thereto, forty per centum ad valorem.

> Old law: On stockings, hose, half-hose, shirts, and drawers, fashioned, narrowed, or shaped wholly or in part by knitting machines or frames, or knit by hand, and composed wholly of cotton, forty per centum ad valorem.

354. Cotton cords, braids, boot, shoe, and corset lacings, thirty-five cents per pound ; cotton gimps, galloons, webbing, goring, suspenders, and braces, any of the foregoing which are elastic or non-elastic, forty per centum ad valorem : *Provided*, That none of the articles included in this paragraph shall pay a less rate of duty than forty per centum ad valorem.

> Old law: Cotton cords, braids, gimps, galloons, webbing, goring, suspenders, braces, thirty-five per centum ad valorem; webbing, not otherwise provided for, thirty-five per centum.

355. Cotton damask, in the piece or otherwise, and all manufactures of cotton not specially provided for in this act, forty per centum ad valorem.

> Old law: Cotton damask, forty per centum; all manufactures not specially provided for, thirty-five per centum.
> Old law: Sail duck or canvas for sails, thirty per centum.

SCHEDULE J.—FLAX, HEMP, AND JUTE, AND MANUFACTURES OF.

356. Flax straw, five dollars per ton.

357. Flax, not hackled or dressed, one cent per pound.

> Old law: Twenty dollars per ton.

358. Flax, hackled, known as "dressed line," three cents per pound.

> Old law: Forty dollars per ton.

359. Tow, of flax or hemp, one half of one cent per pound.

> Old law: Ten dollars per ton.

360. Hemp twenty-five dollars per ton; hemp, hackled, known as line of hemp, fifty dollars per ton.

> Old law: Hemp, manila and other like substitutes for hemp not specially enumerated or provided for in this act, twenty-five dollars per ton.

361. Yarn, made of jute, thirty-five per centum ad valorem.

362. Cables, cordage, and twine (except binding twine, composed in whole or in part of istle or Tampico fiber, manila, sisal grass or sunn), one and one-half cents per pound; all binding twine, manufactured in whole or in part from istle or Tampico fiber, manila, sisal grass, or sunn, seven-tenths of one cent per pound; cables and cordage, made of hemp, two and one-half cents per pound; tarred cables and cordage, three cents per pound.

> Old law: Tarred cables or cordage, three cents per pound; untarred manila cordage, two and one-half cents per pound. All other untarred cordage, three and one-half cents per pound.

363 Hemp and jute carpets and carpetings, six cents per square yard.

364. Burlaps, not exceeding sixty inches in width, of flax, jute or hemp, or of which flax, jute, or hemp, or either of them, shall be the component material of chief value (except such as may be suitable for bagging for cotton), one and five-eighths cents per pound.

> Old law: Burlaps not over sixty inches, thirty per centum. Oilcloth foundations, or floor-cloth canvas, or burlaps exceeding sixty inches in width, made of flax, jute, or hemp, or of which flax, jute, or hemp, or either of them, shall be the component material of chief value, forty per centum ad valorem.
>
> Bags and bagging, and like manufactures, not specially enumerated or provided for in this act (except bagging for cotton), composed wholly or in part of flax, hemp, jute, gunny cloth, gunny bags, or other material, forty per centum ad valorem.

365. Bags for grain made of burlaps, two cents per pound.

> Old law: Forty per centum.

366. Bagging for cotton, gunny cloth, and all similar material suitable for covering cotton, composed in whole or in part of hemp, flax, jute, or jute butts, valued at six cents or less per square yard, one and six-tenths cents per square yard; valued at more than six cents per square yard, one and eight-tenths cents per square yard.

> Old law: Gunny cloth, not bagging, valued at ten cents or less per square yard, three cents per pound; valued at over ten cents per square yard, four cents per pound.
>
> Bagging for cotton, or other manufactures, not specially enumerated or provided for in this act, suitable to the uses for which cotton bagging is applied, composed in whole or in part of hemp, jute, jute butts, flax, gunny bags, gunny cloth, or other material, and valued at seven cents or less per square yard, one and one-half cents per pound; valued at over seven cents per square yard, two cents per pound.

367. Flax gill-netting, nets, webs, and seines, when the thread or twine of which they are composed is made of yarn of a number not higher than twenty, fifteen cents per pound, and thirty-five per centum ad valorem; when made of threads or twines, the yarn of which is finer than number twenty, twenty cents per pound and in addition thereto forty-five per centum ad valorem.

> Text of old law: Seines, and seine and gilling twine, twenty-five per centum.

368. Linen hydraulic hose, made in whole or in part of flax, hemp or jute, twenty cents per pound.

New provision.

369. Oil-cloth for floors, stamped, painted, or printed, *including linoleum, corticene, cork-carpets, figured or plain*, and all other oil-cloth (except silk oil-cloth), and water-proof cloth, not specially provided for in this act, valued at twenty-five cents or less per square yard, forty per centum ad valorem; valued above twenty-five cents per square yard, fifteen cents per square yard and thirty per centum ad valorem.

Old law: Forty per centum.
NOTE.—New matter in italics.

370. Yarns or threads composed of flax or hemp, or of a mixture of either of these substances, valued at thirteen cents or less per pound, six cents per pound; valued at more than thirteen cents per pound, forty-five per centum ad valorem.

Old law: Yarns, thirty-five per centum; flax or linen thread, twine or pack-thread, forty per centum.

371. All manufactures of flax or hemp, or of which these substances, or either of them, is the component material of chief value, not specially provided for in this act, fifty per centum ad valorem : *Provided,* That until January first, eighteen hundred and ninety-four, such manufactures of flax containing more than one hundred threads to the square inch, counting both warp and filling, shall be subject to a duty of thirty-five per centum ad valorem in lieu of the duty herein provided.

Old law: Brown and bleached linens, ducks, canvas, paddings cot-bottoms, diapers, crash, huckabacks, handkerchiefs, lawns, or other manufactures of flax, jute, or hemp, or of which flax, jute, or hemp shall be the component material of chief value not specially enumerated or provided for in this act, thirty-five per centum ad valorem; manufactures of flax of which flax shall be the component material of chief value, not specially provided for, forty per centum. Russia and other sheetings of flax or hemp, brown or white, thirty-five per centum.
Webbings composed of cotton, flax, or any other material, not otherwise provided for, thirty-five per centum.

372. Collars and cuffs, composed entirely of cotton, fifteen cents per dozen pieces and thirty-five per centum ad valorem; composed in whole or in part of linen, thirty cents per dozen pieces and forty-per centum ad valorem; shirts, and all articles of wearing apparel of every description, not specially provided for in this act, composed wholly or in part of linen, fifty-five per centum ad valorem.

New provision. Old law: Rulings of Treasury Department, thirty-five per centum on cotton goods, thirty and forty per centum on linen.

373. Laces, edgings, embroideries, insertings, neck rufflings, ruchings, trimmings, tuckings, lace window-curtains, and other similar tamboured articles, and articles embroidered by hand or machinery, embroidered and hem-stitched handkerchiefs, and articles made wholly or in part of lace, rufflings, tuckings, or ruchings, all of the above-named articles, composed of flax, jute, cotton, or other vegetable fiber, or of which these substances or either of them, or a mixture of any of them is the component material of chief value, not specially provided for in this act, sixty per centum ad valorem : *Provided,* That articles of wearing apparel, and textile fabrics, when embroidered by hand or machinery, and whether specially or otherwise provided for in this act, shall not pay a less rate of duty than that fixed by the respective paragraphs and schedules of this act upon embroideries of the materials of which they are respectively composed.

> Old law: Cotton laces, embroideries, insertings, trimmings, lace window-curtains, forty per centum ad valorem.
> Flax or linen laces and insertings, embroideries, or manufactures of linen, if embroidered or tamboured in the loom or otherwise, by machinery or with the needle or other process, and not specially enumerated or provided for in this act, thirty per centum ad valorem.

374. All manufactures of jute, or other vegetable fiber, except flax, hemp or cotton, or of which jute, or other vegetable fiber, except flax, hemp or cotton, is the component material of chief value, not specially provided for in this act, valued at five cents per pound or less, two cents per pound; valued above five cents per pound, forty per centum ad valorem.

> Old law: All other manufactures of hemp, or manilla, or of which hemp or manilla shall be a component material of chief value, not especially enumerated or provided for in this act, thirty-five per centum ad valorem.
> Grass-cloth and other manufactures of jute, ramie, China, and sisal grass, not specially enumerated or provided for in this act, thirty-five per centum ad valorem.

SCHEDULE K.—WOOL AND MANUFACTURES OF WOOL.

375. All wools, hair of the *camel*, goat, alpaca, and other like animals shall be divided for the purpose of fixing the duties to be charged thereon into the three following classes :

NOTE.—New matter in italics.

376. Class one, that is to say, Merino, mestiza, metz, or metis wools, or other wools of Merino blood, immediate or remote, Down clothing wools, and wools of like character with any of the preceding, including such as have been heretofore usually imported into the United States from Buenos Ayres, New Zealand, Australia, Cape of Good Hope, Russia, Great Britain, Canada, and elsewhere, and also including all wools not hereinafter described or designated in classes two and three.

377. Class two, that is to say, Leicester, Cotswold, Lincolnshire, Down combing wools, Canada long wools, or other like combing wools of English blood, and usually known by the terms herein used, and also hair of the camel, goat, alpaca, and other like animals.

378. Class three, that is to say, Donskoi, native South American, Cordova, Valparaiso, native Smyrna, Russian camels hair, and including all such wools of like character as have been heretofore usually imported into the United States from Turkey, Greece, Egypt, Syria, and elsewhere, excepting improved wools hereinafter provided for.

> Old law: Class three, carpet wools and other similar wools.—Such as Donskoi, native South American, Cordova, Valparaiso, native Smyrna, and including all such wools of like character as have been heretofore usually imported into the United States from Turkey, Greece, Egypt, Syria, and elsewhere.

379. The standard samples of all wools which are now or may be hereafter deposited in the principal custom-houses of the United

States, under the authority of the Secretary of the Treasury, shall be the standards for the classification of wools under this act, and the Secretary of the Treasury shall have the authority to renew these standards and to make such additions to them from time to time as may be required, and he shall cause to be deposited like standards in other custom-houses of the United States when they may be needed.

New provision.

380. Whenever wools of class three shall have been improved by the admixture of Merino or English blood from their present character as represented by the standard samples now or hereafter to be deposited in the principal custom-houses of the United States, such improved wools shall be classified for duty either as class one or as class two, as the case may be.

New provision.

381. The duty on wools of the first class which shall be imported washed shall be twice the amount of the duty to which they would be subjected if imported unwashed; and the duty on wools of the first and second classes which shall be imported scoured shall be three times the duty to which they would be subjected if imported unwashed.

> Old law: The duty on wools of the first class which shall be imported washed shall be twice the amount of the duty to which they would be subjected if imported unwashed; and the duty on wools of all classes which shall be imported scoured shall be three times the duty to which they would be subjected if imported unwashed.

382. Unwashed wools shall be considered such as shall have been shorn from the sheep without any cleansing; that is, in their natural condition. Washed wools shall be considered such as have been washed with water on the sheep's back. Wool washed in any other manner than on the sheep's back shall be considered as scoured wool.

New provision.

383. The duty upon wool of the sheep or hair of the camel, goat, alpaca, and other like animals which shall be imported in any other than ordinary condition, or which shall be changed in its character or condition for the purpose of evading the duty, or which shall be reduced in value by the admixture of dirt, or any other foreign substance, or which has been sorted or increased in value by the rejection of any part of the original fleece, shall be twice the duty to which it would be otherwise subject : *Provided*, That skirted wools as now imported are hereby excepted. Wools on which a duty is assessed amounting to three times or more than that which would be assessed if said wool was imported unwashed, such duty shall not be doubled on account of its being sorted. If any bale or package of wool or hair specified in this act imported as of any specified class, or claimed by the importer to be dutiable as of any specified class, shall contain any wool or hair subject to a higher rate of duty than the class so specified, the whole bale or package shall be subject to the highest rate of duty chargeable on wool of the class subject to such higher rate of duty, and if any bale or package be claimed by the importer to be shoddy, mungo, flocks, wool, hair, or other material of any class specified in this act, and such bale contain any admixture of any one or more of said materials, or of any other

material, the whole bale or package shall be subject to duty at the highest rate imposed upon any article in said bale or package.

> Old law: The duty upon wool of the sheep, or hair of the alpaca, goat, and other like animals, which shall be imported in any other than ordinary condition, as now and heretofore practiced, or which shall be changed in its character or condition for the purpose of evading the duty, or which shall be reduced in value by the admixture of dirt or any other foreign substance, shall be twice the duty to which it would be otherwise subject.

384. The duty upon all wools and hair of the first class shall be eleven cents per pound, and upon all wools or hair of the second class twelve cents per pound.

> Old law: Wools of the first class, the value whereof at the last port or place whence exported to the United States, excluding charges in such port, shall be thirty cents or less per pound, ten cents per pound; wools of the same class, the value whereof at the last port or place whence exported to the United States, excluding charges in such port, shall exceed thirty cents per pound, twelve cents per pound.
>
> Wools of the second class, and all hair of the alpaca, goat, and other like animals, the value whereof, at the last port or place whence exported to the United States, excluding charges in such port, shall be thirty cents or less per pound, ten cents per pound; wools of the same class, the value whereof at the last port or place whence exported to the United States, excluding charges in such port, shall exceed thirty cents per pound, twelve cents per pound.

385. On wools of the third class and on camel's hair of the third class the value whereof shall be thirteen cents or less per pound, including charges, the duty shall be thirty-two per centum ad valorem.

386. On wools of the third class, and on camel's hair of the third class, the value whereof shall exceed thirteen cents per pound including charges, the duty shall be fifty per centum ad valorem.

> Old law: Wools of the third class, the value whereof, at the last port or place whence exported to the United States, excluding charges in such port, shall be twelve cents or less per pound, two and a half cents per pound; wools of the same class, the value whereof, at the last port or place whence exported to the United States, excluding charges in such port, shall exceed twelve cents per pound, five cents per pound.

387. Wools on the skin shall pay the same rate as other wools, the quantity and value to be ascertained under such rules as the Secretary of the Treasury may prescribe.

388. On noils, shoddy, top waste, slubbing waste, roving waste, ring waste, yarn waste, garnetted waste, and all other wastes composed wholly or in part of wool, the duty shall be thirty cents per pound.

> Old law: Shoddy and waste, ten cents per pound.

389. On woolen rags, mungo, and flocks, the duty shall be ten cents per pound.

> Old law: Shoddy and waste have been transferred to preceding paragraph.

390. Wools, and hair of the camel, goat, alpaca, or other like animals, in the form of roping, roving, or tops, and all wool and hair which have been advanced in any manner or by any process of manufacture beyond the washed or scoured condition, not specially provided for in this act, shall be subject to the same duties as are imposed upon manufactures of wool not specially provided for in this act.

> New provision.

391. On woolen and worsted yarns made wholly or in part of wool, worsted, the hair of the camel, goat, alpaca, or other animals, valued at not more than thirty cents per pound, the duty per pound shall be two and one-half times the duty imposed by this act on a pound of unwashed wool of the first class, and in addition thereto, thirty five per centum ad valorem ; valued at more than thirty cents and not more than forty cents per pound, the duty per pound shall be three times the duty imposed by this act on a pound of unwashed wool of the first class, and in addition thereto thirty-five per centum ad valorem ; valued at more than forty cents per pound, the duty per pound shall be three and one-half times the duty imposed by this act on a pound of unwashed wool of the first class, and in addition thereto forty per centum ad valorem.

Old law: For rates, see paragraph 395.

392. On woolen or worsted cloths, shawls, knit fabrics, and all fabrics made on knitting machines or frames, and all manufactures of every description made wholly or in part of wool, worsted, the hair of the camel, goat, alpaca, or other animals, not specially provided for in this act, valued at not more than thirty cents per pound, the duty per pound shall be three times the duty imposed by this act on a pound of unwashed wool of the first class, and in addition thereto forty per centum ad valorem; valued at more than thirty and not more than forty cents per pound, the duty per pound shall be three and one-half times the duty imposed by this act on a pound of unwashed wool of the first class, and in addition thereto forty per centum ad valorem; valued at above forty cents per pound, the duty per pound shall be four times the duty imposed by this act on a pound of unwashed wool of the first class, and in addition thereto fifty per centum ad valorem.

Old law: Woolen cloths, woolen shawls, and all manufactures of wool of every description. made wholly or in part of wool, not specially enumerated or provided for in this act, valued at not exceeding eighty cents per pound, thirty-five cents per pound and thirty-five per centum ad valorem; valued at above eighty cents per pound, thirty-five cents per pound, and in addition thereto forty per centum ad valorem.

393. On blankets, hats of wool, and flannels for underwear composed wholly or in part of wool, the hair of the camel, goat, alpaca, or other animals, valued at not more than thirty cents per pound, the duty per pound shall be the same as the duty imposed by this act on one pound and one-half of unwashed wool of the first class, and in addition thereto thirty per centum ad valorem; valued at more than thirty and not more than forty cents per pound, the duty per pound shall be twice the duty imposed by this act on a pound of unwashed wool of the first class; valued at more than forty cents and not more than fifty cents per pound, the duty per pound shall be three times the duty imposed by this act on a pound of unwashed wool of the first class; and in addition thereto upon all the above-named articles thirty-five per centum ad valorem. On blankets and hats of wool composed wholly or in part of wool, the hair of the camel, goat, alpaca, or other animal, valued at more than fifty cents per pound, the duty per pound shall be three and a half times the duty imposed by this act on a pound of unwashed wool of the first class, and in addition thereto forty per centum ad valorem. Flannels composed wholly or in part of wool, the hair of the camel, goat, alpaca, or other animals, valued at above fifty cents per pound shall

be classified and pay the same duty as women's and children's dress goods, coat lining, Italian cloths, and goods of similar character and description provided by this act.

> Flannels, blankets, hats of wool, knit goods, and all goods made on knitting-frames, balmorals, woolen and worsted yarns, and all manufactures of every description, composed wholly or in part of worsted, the hair of the alpaca, goat, or other animals, (except such as are composed in part of wool), not specially enumerated or provided for in this act, valued at not exceeding thirty cents per pound, ten cents per pound ; valued at above thirty cents per pound, and not exceeding forty cents per pound, twelve cents per pound; valued at above forty cents per pound, and not exceeding sixty cents per pound, eighteen cents per pound; valued at above sixty cents per pound, and not exceeding eighty cents per pound, twenty-four cents per pound; and in addition thereto, upon all the above-named articles thirty-five per centum ad valorem: valued at above eighty cents per pound, thirty-five cents per pound, and in addition thereto forty per centum ad valorem.

394. On women's and children's dress goods, coat linings Italian cloths, and goods of similar character or description of which the warp consists wholly of cotton or other vegetable material, with the remainder of the fabric composed wholly or in part of wool, worsted, the hair of the camel, goat, alpaca, or other animals, valued at not exceeding fifteen cents per square yard, seven cents per square yard, and in addition thereto forty per centum ad valorem; valued at above fifteen cents per square yard, eight cents per square yard, and in addition thereto fifty per centum ad valorem : *Provided*, That on all such goods weighing over four ounces per square yard the duty per pound shall be four times the duty imposed by this act on a pound of unwashed wool of the first class, and in addition thereto fifty per centum ad valorem.

> Old law: Women's and children's dress goods, coat linings, Italian cloths, and goods of like description, composed in part of wool, worsted, the hair of the alpaca, goat, or other animals, valued at not exceeding twenty cents per square yard, five cents per square yard, and in addition thereto thirty-five per centum ad valorem; valued at above twenty cents per square yard, seven cents per square yard, and forty per centum ad valorem: if composed wholly of wool, worsted, the hair of the alpaca, goat, or other animals, or of a mixture of them, nine cents per square yard and forty per centum ad valorem, but all such goods with selvedges, made wholly or in part of other materials, or with threads of other materials introduced for the purpose of changing the classification, shall be dutiable at nine cents per square yard and forty per centum ad valorem: *Provided*, That all such goods weighing over four ounces per square yard shall pay a duty of thirty-five cents per pound and forty per centum ad valorem.

395. On women's and children's dress goods, coat linings. Italian cloth, bunting, and goods of similar description or character composed wholly or in part of wool, worsted, the hair of the camel, goat, alpaca, or other animals, and not specially provided for in this act, the duty shall be twelve cents per square yard, and in addition thereto fifty per centum ad valorem: *Provided*, That on all such goods weighing over four ounces per square yard the duty per pound shall be four times the duty imposed by this act on a pound of unwashed wool of the first class, and in addition thereto fifty per centum ad valorem.

> Old law: See preceding paragraph. Bunting, ten cents per square yard, and in addition thereto, thirty-five per centum ad valorem.

396. On clothing, ready made, and articles of wearing apparel of every description, made up or manufactured wholly or in part, not specially provided for in this act, felts not woven, and not specially provided for in this act, plushes and other pile fabrics, all of the foregoing, composed wholly or in part of wool, worsted, the hair of the camel, goat, alpaca, or other animals the duty per pound shall be four and one-half times the duty imposed by this act on a pound of unwashed wool of the first class, and in addition thereto sixty per centum ad valorem.

> Old law: Clothing, ready-made, and wearing apparel of every description, not specifically enumerated or provided for in this act, and balmoral skirts, and skirting, and goods of similar description, or used for like purposes, composed wholly or in part of wool, worsted, the hair of the alpaca, goat, or other animals, made up or manufactured wholly or in part by the tailor, seamstress, or manufacturer, except knit goods, forty cents per pound, and in addition thereto, thirty-five per centum ad valorem; endless belts or felts for paper or printing machines, twenty cents per pound and thirty per centum ad valorem.

397. On cloaks, dolmans, jackets, talmas, ulsters, or other outside garments for ladies and children's apparel and goods of similar description, or used for like purposes, composed wholly or in part of wool, worsted, the hair of the camel, goat, alpaca, or other animals, made up or manufactured wholly or in part, the duty per pound shall be four and one-half times the duty imposed by this act on a pound of unwashed wool of the first class, and in addition thereto sixty per centum ad valorem.

> Old law: Cloaks, dolmans, jackets, talmas, ulsters, or other outside garments for ladies' and children's apparel and goods of similar description, or used for like purposes, composed wholly or in part of wool, worsted, the hair of the alpaca, goat, or other animals, made up or manufactured wholly or in part by the tailor, seamstress, or manufacturer (except knit goods), forty-five cents per pound, and in addition thereto forty per centum ad valorem.

398. On webbings, gorings, suspenders, braces, beltings, bindings, braids, galloons, fringes, gimps, cords, cords and tassels, dress trimmings, laces and embroideries, head nets, buttons, or barrel buttons, or buttons of other forms, for tassels or ornaments, wrought by hand or braided by machinery any of the foregoing which are elastic or non-elastic, made of wool, worsted, the hair of the camel, goat, alpaca, or other animals, or of which wool, worsted, the hair of the camel, goat, alpaca, or other animals is a component material, the duty shall be sixty cents per pound, and in addition thereto sixty per centum ad valorem.

> Webbings, gorings, suspenders, braces, beltings, bindings, braids, galloons, fringes, gimps, cords and tassels, dress-trimmings, head-nets, buttons, or barrel buttons, or buttons of other forms for tassels or ornaments, wrought by hand, or braided by machinery, made of wool, worsted, the hair of the alpaca, goat, or other animals, or of which wool, worsted, the hair of the alapaca, goat, or other animals is a component material, thirty cents per pound, and in addition thereto, fifty per centum ad valorem.

399. Aubusson, Axminster, Moquette, and Chenille carpets, figured or plain, carpets woven whole for rooms, and all carpets or carpeting of like character or description, and oriental, Berlin, and other similar rugs, sixty cents per square yard, and in addition thereto forty per centum ad valorem.

> Old law: Forty-five cents per square yard and thirty per centum ad valorem.

400. Saxony, Wilton, and Tournay velvet carpets, figured or plain, and all carpets or carpeting of like character or description, sixty cents per square yard, and in addition thereto forty per centum ad valorem.

> Old law: Forty-five cents square yard and thirty per centum ad valorem.

401. Brussels carpets, figured or plain, and all carpets or carpeting of like character or description, forty-four cents per square yard, and in addition thereto forty per centum ad valorem.

> Old law: Thirty cents square yard and thirty per centum ad valorem.

402. Velvet and tapestry velvet carpets, figured or plain, printed on the warp or otherwise, and all carpets or carpeting of like character or description, forty cents per square yard, and in addition thereto forty per centum ad valorem.

> Old law: Twenty-five cents square yard and thirty per centum ad valorem.

403. Tapestry Brussels carpets, figured or plain, and all carpets or carpeting of like character or description, printed on the warp or otherwise, twenty-eight cents per square yard, and in addition thereto forty per centum ad valorem.

> Old law: Twenty cents square yard and thirty per centum ad valorem.

404. Treble ingrain, three-ply, and all chain Venetian carpets, nineteen cents per square yard, and in addition thereto forty per centum ad valorem.

> Old law: Twelve cents per square yard and thirty per centum.

405. Wool Dutch and two-ply ingrain carpets, fourteen cents per square yard, and in addition thereto forty per centum ad valorem.

> Old law: Eight cents per square yard and thirty per centum.

406. Druggets and bockings, printed, colored, or otherwise, twenty-two cents per square yard, and in addition thereto forty per centum ad valorem. Felt carpeting, figured or plain, eleven cents per square yard, and in addition thereto forty per centum ad valorem.

> Old law: Druggets and bockings fifteen cents per square yard and thirty per centum; felt carpeting, fifteen cents per square yard and thirty per centum, by ruling of Treasury Department.

407. Carpets and carpenting of wool, flax or cotton, or composed in part of either, not specially provided for in this act, fifty per centum ad valorem.

> Old law: Carpets and carpetings of wool, flax, or cotton, or parts of either or other material, not otherwise herein specified, forty per centum ad valorem.

408. Mats, rugs, screens, covers, hassocks, bed sides, art squares, and other portions of carpets or carpeting made wholly or in part of wool, and not specially provided for in this act, shall be subjected to the rate of duty herein imposed on carpets or carpetings of like character or description.

> Old law: Mats, rugs, screens, covers, hassocks, bedsides, and other portions of carpets or carpetings, shall be subjected to the rate of duty herein imposed on carpets or carpeting of like character or description; and the duty on all other mats not exclusively of vegetable material, screens, hassocks, and rugs, shall be forty per centum ad valorem.

Schedule L.—Silk and Silk Goods.

409. Silk partially manufactured from cocoons or from waste-silk, and not further advanced or manufactured than carded or combed silk, fifty cents per pound.

410. Thrown silk, not more advanced than singles, tram, organzine, sewing silk, twist, floss, and silk threads or yarns of every description; except spun silk, thirty per centum ad valorem; spun silk in skeins or cops or on beams, thirty-five per centum ad valorem.

Old law: All this paragraph thirty-five per centum.

411. Velvets, plushes, or other pile fabrics, containing, exclusive of selvedges, less than seventy-five per centum in weight of silk, one dollar and fifty cents per pound and fifteen per centum ad valorem; containing, exclusive of selvedges, seventy-five per centum or more in weight of silk, three dollars and fifty cents per pound, and fifteen per centum ad valorem: but in no case shall any of the foregoing articles pay a less rate of duty than fifty per centum ad valorem.

New provision. Old law: Classified as manufactures at fifty per centum.

412. Webbings, gorings, suspenders, braces, beltings, bindings, braids, galloons, fringes, cords and tassels, any of the foregoing which are elastic or non-elastic, buttons, and ornaments, made of silk, or of which silk is the component material of chief value, fifty per centum ad valorem.

New provision. Old law: Classified as manufactures at fifty per centum.

413. Laces and embroideries, handkerchiefs, neck rufflings and ruchings, clothing ready-made, and articles of wearing apparel of every description, including knit goods, made up or manufactured wholly or in part by the tailor, seamtress, or manufacturer, composed of silk, or of which silk is the component material, of chief value, not specially provided for in this act, sixty per centum ad valorem: *Provided,* That all such clothing ready made and articles of wearing apparel when composed in part of India rubber (not including gloves or elastic articles that are specially provided for in this act), shall be subject to a duty of eight cents per ounce, and in addition thereto sixty per centum ad valorem.

New provision. Old law: Classified as manufactures at fifty per centum.

414. All manufactures of silk, or of which silk is the component material of chief value, not specially provided for in this act, fifty per centum ad valorem: *Provided,* That all such manufactures of which wool, or the hair of the camel, goat, or other like animals is a component material, shall be classified as manufactures of wool.

Old law: All goods, wares, and merchandise, not specially enumerated or provided for in this act, made of silk, or of which silk is the component material of chief value, fifty per centum ad valorem.

Schedule M.—Pulp, Papers, and Books,

Pulp and Paper.—

415. Mechanically ground wood pulp two dollars and fifty cents per ton dry weight; chemical wood pulp unbleached, six dollars per ton dry weight; bleached, seven dollars per ton dry weight.

Old law: Pulp dried for paper-makers' use, ten per centum.

416. Sheathing paper, ten per centum ad valorem.

417. Printing paper unsized, suitable only for books and news-papers, fifteen per centum ad valorem.

> Slight change in text.

418. Printing paper sized or glued, suitable only for books and newspapers, twenty per centum ad valorem.

> Old law: Limited to printing papers.

419. Papers known commercially as copying paper, filtering paper, silver paper, and all tissue paper, white or colored, whether made up in copying books, reams, or in any other form, eight cents per pound, and in addition thereto fifteen per centum ad valorem; albumenized or sensitized paper, thirty-five per centum ad valorem.

> Old law : Blank-books for press copying twenty per centum ; on all other of above paragraph twenty-five per centum as manu-factures of paper.

420. Papers known commercially as surface-coated papers, and manufactures thereof, card-boards, lithographic prints from either stone or zinc, bound or unbound (except illustrations when forming a part of a periodical, newspaper, or in printed books accompanying the same), and all articles produced either in whole or in part by lithographic process, and photograph, autograph, and scrap albums, wholly or partially manufactured, thirty-five per centum ad volorem.

> Old law: Paper boxes and all other fancy boxes, if of surface-coated papers, principally twenty-five per centum.
> Paper-hangings and paper for screens or fire-boards, paper anti-quarian, demy, drawing, elephant, foolscap, imperial, letter, note, and all other paper not specially enumerated or provided for in this act, twenty-five per centum ad valorem.

MANUFACTURES OF PAPER—

421. Paper envelopes, twenty-five cents per thousand.

> Old law: Twenty-five per centum.

422. Paper hangings and paper for screens or fire-boards, writing-paper, drawing-paper, and all other paper not specially provided for in this act, twenty-five per centum ad valorem.

> Change of text.

423. Books, including blank books of all kinds, pamphlets and en-gravings, bound or unbound, photographs, etchings, maps, charts, and all printed matter not specially provided for in this act, twenty-five per centum ad valorem.

> Old law: Illustrated books twenty-five per centum; blank books, bound, or unbound, twenty per centum.

424. Playing cards, fifty cents per pack

> Old law: One hundred per centum.

425. Manufactures of paper, or of which paper is the component material of chief value, not specially provided for in this act, twenty-five per centum ad valorem.

> Old law: Fifteen per centum, also twenty-five per centum ; paper boxes and all other fancy boxes, thirty-five per centum.

SCHEDULE N.—SUNDRIES.

426. Bristles, ten cents per pound.

> Old law: Fifteen cents per pound.

427. Brushes, and brooms of all kinds, including feather dusters and hair pencils in quills, forty per centum ad valorem.

Old law: Brushes, thirty per centum ; brooms, twenty-five per centum ; hair pencils, thirty per centum.

BUTTONS AND BUTTON FORMS.—

428. Button forms : Lastings, mohair, cloth, silk, or other manufactures of cloth, woven or made in patterns of such size, shape, or form, or cut in such manner as to be fit for buttons exclusively, ten per centum ad valorem.

429. Buttons commercially known as Agate buttons, twenty-five per centum ad valorem. Pearl and shell buttons, two and one-half cents per line button measure of one-fortieth of one inch per gross, and in addition thereto twenty-five per centum ad valorem.

Old law: Buttons and button-molds, not specially enumerated or provided for in this act, not including brass, gilt, or silk buttons, twenty-five per centum ad valorem. Pearl and shell buttons as manufactures of shell, twenty-five per centum.

430. Ivory, vegetable ivory, bone or horn buttons, fifty per centum ad valorem.

Old law: See preceding paragraph.

431. Shoe-buttons, made of paper, board, papier maché, pulp, or other similar material not specially provided for in this act, valued at not exceeding three cents per gross, one cent per gross.

Old law: Not enumerated, at twenty-five per centum.

432. Coal, bituminous, and shale, seventy-five cents per ton of twenty-eight bushels, eighty pounds to the bushel; coal slack or culm, such as will pass through a half-inch screen, thirty cents per ton of twenty-eight bushels, eighty pounds to the bushel.

433. Coke, twenty per centum ad valorem.

434. Cork bark, cut into squares or cubes, ten cents per pound; manufactured corks, fifteen cents per pound.

Old law: Twenty-five per centum.

435. Dice, draughts, chess-men, chess-balls, and billiard, *pool*, and bagatelle balls, of ivory, bone, *or other materials*, fifty per centum ad valorem.

NOTE.—New matter in italics.

436. Dolls, doll-heads, toy marbles of whatever material composed, and all other toys not composed of rubber, china, porcelain, parian, bisque, earthen or stoneware, and not specially provided for in this act, thirty-five per centum ad valorem.

Old law: Dolls and toys, thirty-five per centum.

437. Emery grains, and emery manufactured, ground, pulverized, or refined, one cent per pound.

EXPLOSIVE SUBSTANCES.—

438. Fire-crackers of all kinds, eight cents per pound, *but no allowance shall be made for tare or damage thereon.*

Old law: One hundred per centum; new matter in italics.

439. Fulminates, fulminating powders, and like articles, not specially provided for in this act, thirty per centum ad valorem.

440. Gunpowder, and all explosive substances used for mining, blasting, artillery, or sporting purposes, when valued at

twenty cents or less per pound, five cents per pound : valued above twenty cents per pound, eight cents per pound.

Old law: Six and eight cents.

441. Matches, friction or lucifer, of all descriptions, per gross of one hundred and forty-four boxes, containing not more than one hundred matches per box, ten cents per gross; when imported otherwise than in boxes containing not more than one hundred matches each, one cent per one thousand matches.

Old law: Friction or lucifer matches of all descriptions, thirty-five per centum.

442. Percussion-caps, forty per centum ad valorem.

443. Feathers and downs of all kinds, crude or not dressed, colored, or manufactured, not specially provided for in this act, ten per centum ad valorem; when dressed, colored, or manufactured, including quilts of down and other manufactures of down, and also including dressed and finished birds suitable for millinery ornaments, and artificial and ornamental feathers and flowers, or parts thereof, of whatever material composed, not specially provided for in this act, fifty per centum ad valorem.

Old law: Feathers of all kinds, crude, or not dressed, colored, or manufactured, twenty-five per centum ad valorem; when dressed, colored, or manufactured, including dressed and finished birds, for millinery ornaments, and artificial and ornamental feathers and flowers, or parts thereof, of whatever material composed, for millinery use, not specially enumerated or provided for in this act, fifty per centum ad valorem.

444. Furs, dressed on the skin *but not made up into articles*, and furs not on the skin, prepared for hatters' use, twenty per centum ad valorem.

NOTE.—New matter in italics.

445. Glass beads, loose, unthreaded or unstrung, ten per centum ad valorem.

Old law: Beads and bead ornaments of all kinds, except amber, fifty per centum.

446. Gun-wads of all descriptions, thirty-five per centum ad valorem.

447. Hair, human, if clean or drawn but not manufactured, twenty per centum ad valorem.

Old law: Thirty per centum.

448. Hair-cloth, known as "crinoline-cloth," eight cents per square yard.

Old law: Thirty per centum.

449. Hair-cloth, known as "hair seating," thirty cents per square yard.

450. Hair, curled, suitable for beds or mattresses, fifteen per centum ad valorem.

Old law: Curled hair, except of hogs, used for beds or mattresses, twenty-five per centum.

451. Hats, for men's, women's, and children's wear, composed of the fur of the rabbit, beaver, or other animals or of which such fur is the component material of chief value, wholly or partially manufactured, including fur hat bodies, fifty-five per centum ad valorem.

Old law: Twenty per centum by Treasury ruling: bonnets, hats, and hoods of hair, not specially provided for, thirty per centum.

JEWELRY AND PRECIOUS STONES.—

452. Jewelry : All articles, not elsewhere specially provided for in this act composed of precious metals or imitations thereof, whether set with coral, jet, or pearls, or with diamonds, rubies, cameos, or other precious stones, or imitations thereof, or otherwise, and which shall be known commercially as "jewelry," and cameos in frames, fifty per centum ad valorem.

Old law : Jewelry of all kinds, twenty-five per centum.

453. Pearls, ten per centum ad valorem.

Old law : Classified at ten per centum and fifty per centum ad valorem.

454. Precious stones of all kinds, cut but not set, ten per centum ad valorem ; if set, and not specially provided for in this act, twenty-five per centum ad valorem. Imitations of precious stones composed of paste or glass not exceeding one inch in dimensions, not set, ten per centum ad valorem.

Old law : Precious stones of all kinds, ten per centum; compositions of glass or paste when not set, ten per centum.

LEATHER AND MANUFACTURES OF.—

455. Bend or belting leather and sole leather, and leather not specially provided for in this act, ten per centum ad valorem.

Old law : Leather, bend or belting leather, and Spanish or other sole leather, and leather not specially enumerated or provided for in this act, fifteen per centum ad valorem.

456. Calf-skins, tanned, or tanned and dressed, dressed upper leather, including patent, enameled, and japanned leather, dressed or undressed, and finished; chamois or other skins not specially enumerated or provided for in this act, twenty per centum ad valorem ; book-binders' calf-skins, kangaroo, sheep and goat skins, including lamb and kid skins, dressed and finished, twenty per centum ad valorem ; skins for morocco, tanned but unfinished, ten per centum ad valorem ; piano forte leather and piano forte action leather, thirty five per centum ad valorem ; japanned calf-skins, thirty per centum ad valorem ; boots and shoes, made of leather, twenty five per centum ad valorem.

457. But leather cut into shoe uppers or vamps, or other forms, suitable for conversion into manufactured articles, shall be classified as manufactures of leather, and pay duty accordingly.

Calfskins, tanned, or tanned and dressed, and dressed upper leather of all other kinds, and skins dressed and finished, of all kinds, not specially enumerated or provided for in this act, and skins of morocco, finished, twenty per centum ad valorem.

Skins for morocco, tanned, but unfinished, ten per centum ad valorem.

All manufactures and articles of leather, or of which leather shall be a component part, not specially enumerated or provided for in this act, thirty per centum ad valorem.

458. Gloves of all descriptions, composed wholly or in part of kid or other leather, and whether wholly or partly manufactured, shall pay duty at the rates fixed in connection with the following specified kinds thereof, fourteen inches in extreme length when stretched to the full extent, being in each case hereby fixed as the standard, and one dozen pairs as the basis, namely : Ladies' and children's schmaschen of said

length or under, one dollar and seventy-five cents per dozen; ladies' and children's lamb of said length or under, two dollars and twenty-five cents per dozen; ladies' and children's kid of said length or under, three dollars and twenty-five cents per dozen; ladies' and children's suedes of said length or under, fifty per centum ad valorem; all other ladies' and children's leather gloves, and all men's leather gloves of said length or under, fifty per centum ad valorem; all leather gloves over fourteen inches in length, fifty per centum ad valorem; and in addition to the above rates there shall be paid on all men's gloves one dollar per dozen; on all lined gloves one dollar per dozen; on all pique or prick seam gloves, fifty cents per dozen; on all embroidered gloves, with more than three single strands or cords, fifty cents per dozen pairs. *Provided*, That all gloves represented to be of a kind or grade below their actual kind or grade shall pay an additional duty of five dollars per dozen pairs: *Provided further*, That none of the articles named in this paragraph shall pay a less rate of duty than fifty per centum ad valorem.

> Old law: Gloves, kid or leather, of all descriptions, wholly or partially manufactured, fifty per centum ad valorem.

MISCELLANEOUS MANUFACTURES.—

459. Manufactures of alabaster, amber, asbestos, bladders, coral, cat-gut or whip-gut or worm-gut, jet, paste, spar, wax, or of which these substances or either of them is the component material of chief value, not specially provided for in this act, twenty-five per centum ad valorem; osier or willow prepared for basketmakers' use, thirty per centum ad valorem; manufactures of osier or willow, forty per centum ad valorem.

> Old law: Baskets and all other articles composed of osier, or willow, not specially enumerated or provided for in this act, thirty per centum ad valorem.
>
> Alabaster and spar statuary and ornaments, ten per centum; manufactures of bladders, twenty-five per centum; bonnets, hats, and hoods for men, women, and children, composed of willow, thirty per centum; wax candles and tapers, twenty per centum; willow sheets or squares, twenty per centum; osier or willow prepared for basketmakers' use, twenty-five per centum; gut and worm-gut, manufactures, free; asbestos, manufactures, twenty-five per centum; jet manufactures and imitations of, twenty-five per centum.

460. Manufactures of bone, chip, grass, horn, India-rubber, palm-leaf, straw, weeds, or whale-bone, or of which these substances or either of them is the component material of chief value, not specially provided for in this act, thirty per centum ad valorem.

> Old law: Manufactures of bone and horn, compositions of, thirty per centum; paste, ten per centum; coral, cut, manufactured, twenty-five per centum; baskets and all other articles composed of grass, palm-leaf, whalebone, or straw, thirty per centum.
>
> India-rubber fabrics, composed wholly or in part of India rubber, not specially enumerated or provided for in this act, thirty per centum ad valorem.
>
> Articles composed of India rubber, not specially enumerated or provided for in this act, twenty-five per centum ad valorem.
>
> India-rubber boots and shoes, twenty-five per centum ad valorem.

Bonnets, hats, and hoods for men, women, and children, composed of chip, grass, palm-leaf, or straw, or any other vegetable substance, whalebone, or other material, not specially enumerated or provided for in this act, thirty per centum ad valorem.

461. Manufactures of leather, fur, gutta-percha, vulcanized India rubber, known as hard rubber, human hair, papier-mache, and indurated fiber wares and other manufactures composed of wood or other pulp, or of which these substances or either of them is the component material of chief value, all of the above not specially provided for in this act, thirty-five per centum ad valorem.

> Old law: Fur, articles of, thirty per centum; human hair, when manufactured, thirty-five per centum; gutta-percha, manufactured, and all articles of, thirty-five per centum; papier-mache manufactures, articles and wares, thirty per centum.
> Hair, human, bracelets, braids, chains, rings, curls, and ringlets, composed of hair, or of which hair is the component material of chief value, thirty-five per centum ad valorem.

462. Manufactures of ivory, vegetable ivory, mother-of-pearl, and shell, or of which these substances or either of them is the component material of chief value, not specially provided for in this act, forty per centum ad valorem.

> Old law: Manufactures of ivory and vegetable ivory, thirty per centum; shells, whole or parts of, manufactured, of every description not specially provided for, twenty-five per centum ad valorem.

463. Masks, composed of paper or pulp, thirty-five per centum ad valorem.

> New provision.

464. Matting made of cocoa-fiber or rattan, twelve cents per square yard; mats made of cocoa-fiber or rattan, eight cents per square foot.

> Old law: Floor matting and floor mats, exclusively of vegetable substances, twenty per centum,

465. Paintings, in oil or water colors, and statuary, not otherwise provided for in this act, fifteen per centum ad valorem; but the term "statuary" as herein used shall be understood to include only such statuary as is cut, carved, or otherwise wrought by hand from a solid block or mass of marble, stone, or alabaster, or from metal, and as is the professional production of a statuary or sculptor only.

> Old law: Thirty per centum.

466. Pencils of wood filled with lead or other material, and pencils of lead, fifty cents per gross and thirty per centum ad valorem; slate pencils, four cents per gross.

> Old law: Slate-pencils, thirty per centum.

467. Pencil-leads not in wood, ten per centum ad valorem.

PIPES AND SMOKERS' ARTICLES.—

468. Pipes, pipe-bowls, of all materials, and all smokers' articles whatsoever, not specially provided for in this act, including cigarette-books, cigarette book-covers, pouches for smoking or chewing tobacco, and cigarette-paper in all forms, seventy per centum ad valorem; all common tobacco pipes of clay, fifteen cents per gross.

> Pipes, pipe-bowls, and all smokers' articles whatsoever, not specially enumerated or provided for in this act, seventy per centum ad valorem; all common pipes of clay, thirty-five per centum ad valorem.

469. *Plush, black, known commercially as* hatters' plush, composed of silk, or of silk and cotton, *and used exclusively for making men's hats,* ten per centum ad valorem.

> Old law: Twenty-five per centum.
> Note.—New matter in italics.

470. Umbrellas, parasols, and sun-shades covered with silk, or alpaca, fifty-five per centum ad valorem ; if covered with other material, forty-five per centum ad valorem.

> Old law: Fifty per centum and forty per centum.

471. Umbrellas, parasols, and sunshades, sticks for, *if plain,* finished or unfinished, thirty-five per centum ad valorem ; *if carved,* fifty per centum ad valorem.

> Old law: Thirty per centum.

472. Waste, not specially provided for in this act, ten per centum ad valorem.

> Old law: Items specially provided for under the old law, which will be classified under the new law according to the component material of chief value:
>
> Card-cases, pocket-books, shell-boxes, and all similar articles, of whatever material composed, and by whatever name known, not specially enumerated or provided for in this act, thirty-five per centum ad valorem.
>
> Carriages, and parts of, not specially enumerated or provided for in this act, thirty-five per centum ad valorem.
>
> Coach and harness furniture of all kinds, saddlery, coach, and harness hardware, silver-plated, brass, brass-plated, or covered, common, tinned, burnished, or japanned, not specially enumerated or provided for in this act, thirty-five per centum ad valorem.
>
> Combs, of all kinds, thirty per centum ad valorem.
>
> Crayons of all kinds, twenty per centum ad valorem.
>
> Fans of all kinds, except common palm-leaf fans, of whatever material composed, thirty-five per centum ad valorem.
>
> Finishing powder, twenty per centum ad valorem.
>
> Japanned ware of all kinds, not specially enumerated or provided for in this act, forty per centum ad valorem.
>
> Musical instruments of all kinds, twenty-five per centum ad valorem.
>
> Philosophical apparatus and instruments, thirty-five per centum ad valorem.
>
> Polishing powders of every description, by whatever name known, including Frankfort black, and Berlin, Chinese, fig, and wash blue, twenty per centum ad valorem.
>
> Scagliola, and composition tops for tables or for other articles of furniture, thirty-five per centum ad valorem.
>
> Teeth, manufactured, twenty per centum ad valorem.

Free List.

Sec 2. On and after the sixth day of October, eighteen hundred and ninety, unless otherwise specially provided for in this act, the following articles when imported shall be exempt from duty :

473. Acids used for medicinal, chemical, or manufacturing purposes, not specially provided for in this act.

474. Aconite.

475. Acorns, raw, dried or undried, but unground.

476. Agates, unmanufactured.

477. Albumen.

478. Alizarine, natural or artificial, *and dyes commercially known as Alizarine yellow, Alizarine orange, Alizarine green, Alizarine blue, Alizarine brown, Alizarine black.*

> Note.—Italics represent new matter.

479. Amber, unmanufactured, or crude gum.

Old law: Amber beads and gum.

480. Ambergris.

481. Aniline salts,

Old law: Aniline salts, or black salts or black tares.

482. Any animal imported specially for breeding purposes shall be admitted free: *Provided,* That no such animal shall be admitted free unless pure bred of a recognized breed, and duly registered in the book of record established for that breed: *And provided further,* That certificate of such record and of the pedigree of such animal shall be produced and submitted to the customs officer, duly authenticated by the proper custodian of such book of record, together with the affidavit of the owner, agent, or importer that such animal is the identical animal described in said certificate of record and pedigree. The Secretary of the Treasury may prescribe such additional regulations as may be required for the strict enforcement of this provision.

Old law: Animals specially imported for breeding purposes, shall be admitted free upon proof thereof satisfactory to the Secretary of the Treasury, and under such regulations as he may prescribe ; and teams of animals, including their harness and tackle and the vehicles or wagons actually owned by persons emigrating from foreign countries to the United States with their families, and in actual use for the purpose of such emigration, shall also be admitted free of duty, under such regulations as the Secretary of the Treasury may prescribe.

483. Animals brought into the United States temporarily for a period not exceeding six months, for the purpose of exhibition or competition for prizes offered by any agricultural or racing association; but a bond shall be given in accordance with regulations prescribed by the Secretary of the Treasury; also, teams of animals, including their harness and tackle and the wagons or other vehicles actually owned by persons emigrating from foreign countries to the United States with their families, and in actual use for the purpose of such emigration under such regulations as the Secretary of the Treasury may prescribe; *and wild animals intended for exhibition in zoological collections for scientific and educational purposes, and not for sale or profit.*

NOTE.—New matter in italics.

484. Annatto, roucou, rocoa, or orleans, and all extracts of.

485. Antimony ore, crude sulphite of.

486. Apatite.

487. Argal, or argol, or crude tartar.

488. Arrow root, *raw or unmanufactured.*

NOTE.—Words in italics represent new matter.

489. Arsenic and sulphide of, or orpiment.

490. Arseniate of aniline.

491. Art educational stops, composed of glass and metal and valued at not more than six cents per gross.

New provision.

492. Articles in a crude state used in dyeing or tanning not specially provided for in this act.

493. Articles the growth, produce, and manufacture of the United States, when returned after having been exported, without having been advanced in value or improved in condition by any process of manufacture or other means; casks, barrels, carboys, bags, and other vessels of American manufacture exported filled with American products, or exported empty and returned filled with foreign products, including shooks when returned as barrels or boxes; also quicksilver flasks or bottles, of either domestic or foreign manufacture, which shall have been actually exported from the United States; but proof of the identity of such articles shall be made, under general regulations to be prescribed by the Secretary of the Treasury; and if any such articles are subject to internal tax at the time of exportation such tax shall be proved to have been paid before exportation and not refunded: *Provided,* That this paragraph shall not apply to any article upon which an allowance of drawback has been made, the re-importation of which is hereby prohibited except upon payment of duties equal to the drawbacks allowed; or to any article manufactured in bonded-warehouse and exported under any provision of law: *And provided further,* That when manufactured tobacco which has been exported without payment of internal-revenue tax shall be re-imported it shall be retained in the custody of the collector of customs until internal-revenue stamps in payment of the legal duties shall be placed thereon.

> Old law: Barrels of American manufacture, exported filled with domestic petroleum, and returned empty, under such regulations as the Secretary of the Treasury may prescribe, and without requiring the filing of a declaration at time of export of intent to return the same empty.
>
> Articles the growth, produce, and manufacture of the United States, when returned in the same condition as exported. Casks, barrels, barboys, bags, and other vessels of American manufacture, exported filled with American products, or exported empty and returned filled with foreign products, including shooks when returned as barrels or boxes ; but proof of the identity of such articles shall be made under the regulations to be prescribed by the Secretary of the Treasury ; and if any such articles are subject to internal tax at the time of exportation, such tax shall be proved to have been paid before exportation and not refunded. [*a. And provided further,* That bags, other than of American manufacture, in which grain shall have been actually exported from the United States, may be returned empty to the United States, free of duty, under regulations to be prescribed by the Secretary of the Treasury. Sec. 7, act of February 8, 1875.]

494. Asbestos, unmanufactured.

> Old law: Articles imported for the use of the United States, provided that the price of the same did not include the duty.

495. Ashes, wood and lye of, and beet-root ashes.

496. Asphaltum and bitumen, crude.

497. Asafetida.

498. Balm of Gilead.

499. Barks, cinchona or other from which quinine may be extracted.

> Old law: Barks, cinchona or other barks used in the manufacture of quinine.

500. Baryta, carbonate of, or witherite.

501. Bauxite, or beauxite.

502. Beeswax.

> Old law: Twenty per centum.

503. Bells, broken, and bell metal broken and fit only to be remanufactured.

504, Birds, stuffed, *not suitable for millinery ornaments, and bird skins, prepared for preservation, but not further advanced in manufacture.*

NOTE.—Italics represent new matter.

505. Birds and land and water fowls.

506. Bismuth.

507. Bladders, including fish-bladders or fish-sounds, crude, and all integuments of animals not specially provided for in this act.

508. Blood, dried.

509. Bologna sausages.

510. Bolting-cloths, *especially for milling purposes, but not suitable for the manufacture of wearing apparel.*

NOTE.—Italics represents new matter.

511. Bones, crude, or not burned, calcined, ground, steamed, or otherwise manufactured, and bone-dust or animal carbon, and bone ash, fit only for fertilizing purposes.

Old law: Bones, crude, not manufactured, burned, calcined, ground, or steamed.
Bone-dust and bone-ash for manufacture of phosphate and fertilizers.

512. Books, engravings, *photographs,* bound or unbound etchings, maps, and charts, which shall have been printed and *bound* or manufactured more than twenty years at the date of importation.

NOTE.—Italics represent new matter.

513. Books and pamphlets printed exclusively in languages other than English; also books and music, in raised print, used exclusively by the blind.

514. Books, *engravings, photographs, etchings, bound or unbound,* maps and charts imported by authority or for the use of the United States or for the use of the Library of Congress.

NOTE.—Italics indicate new matter. The following words are omitted from new law: " But the duty shall not have been included in the contract of price paid."

515. Books, maps, *lithographic prints,* and charts, specially imported, not more than two copies in any one invoice, in good faith, for the use of any society incorporated or established for *educational,* philosophical, literary, or religious purposes, or for the encouragement of the fine arts, or for the use or by order of any college, academy, school, or seminary of learning in the United States, *subject to such regulations as the Secretary of the Treasury shall prescribe.*

NOTE.—Italics represent new matter.

516. Books, or libraries, or parts of libraries, and other household effects of persons or families from foreign countries, if actually used abroad by them not less than one year, and not intended for any other person or persons, nor for sale.

517. Brazil paste.

518. Braids, plaits, laces, and similar manufactures, composed of straw, chip, grass, palm-leaf, willow, osier, or rattan, suitable for making or ornamenting hats, bonnets, and hoods.

Old law: Twenty per centum.

519. Brazilian pebble, unwrought or unmanufactured.

Old law: Brazilian pebbles for spectacles and pebbles for spectacles rough.

520. Breccia, in block or slabs.

521. Bromine.
522. Bullion, gold or silver.
523. Burgundy pitch.
524. Cabinets of old coins and medals, and other collections of antiquities, but the term " antiquities " as used in this act shall include only such articles as are suitable for souvenirs or cabinet collections, and which shall have been produced at any period prior to the year seventeen hundred.

> Old law: Cabinets of coins, medals, and all other collections of antiquities.

525. Cadmium.
526. Calamine.
527. Camphor, crude.
528. Castor or castoreum.
529. Catgut, whip-gut, or worm-gut, unmanufactured, or not further manufactured than in strings or cords.

> Old law: Catgut strings or gut cord for musical instruments: strings: All strings of catgut or any other like material, other than strings for musical instruments, twenty-five per centum ad valorem.

530. Cerium.
531. Chalk, unmanufactured.

> Old law contains cliffstone.

532. Charcoal.
533 Chicory-root, raw, dried, or undried, but unground.
534 Civet, crude.
535 Clay—Common blue clay in casks suitable for the manufacture of crucibles.

> New provision.

536. Coal, anthracite.
537. Coal stores of American vessels ; but none shall be unloaded.
538. Coal-tar, crude.
539. Cobalt and cobalt-ore.

> Old law: Cobalt, ore of; cobalt as metallic arsenic.

540 Cocculus indicus.
541. Cochineal.
542. Cocoa, or cacao, crude, and fiber, leaves, and shells of.
543. Coffee.
544. Coins, gold, silver, and copper.
545 Coir, and coir yarn.
546. Copper, old, taken from the bottom of American vessels compelled by marine disaster to repair in foreign ports.
547. Coral, marine, *uncut, and* unmanufactured.

> NOTE.—Italics represent new matter.

548. Cork-wood, or cork-bark, unmanufactured.
549. Cotton, *and cotton-waste or flocks.*

> NOTE.—Italics represent new matter.

550. Cryolite, or kryolith.
551. Cudbear.
552. Curling-stones, or quoits, and curling-stone handles.
553. Curry, and curry-powder.
554. Cutch.
555. Cuttle-fish bone.
556. Dandelion roots, raw, dried, or undried, but unground.

88

557. Diamonds *and other precious stones*, rough or uncut, *including glaziers' and engravers' diamonds not set*, and diamond dust or bort, *and jewels to be used in the manufacture of watches.*
558 Divi-divi. •
559. Dragon's blood.
560. Drugs, such as barks, beans, berries, balsams, buds, bulbs, and bulbous roots, excrescences such as nut-galls, fruits, flowers, dried fibers, and dried insects, grains, gums, and gum-resin, herbs, leaves, lichens, mosses, nuts, roots, and stems, spices, vegetables, seeds aromatic, and seeds of morbid growth, weeds, and woods used expressly for dyeing; any of the foregoing which are not edible and are in a crude state, and not advanced in value or condition by refining or grinding, or by other process of manufacture, and not specially provided for in this act.
561. Eggs *of birds, fish, and insects.*
NOTE.—New matter in italics.
562. Emery ore.
563. Ergot.
564. Fans, common palm-leaf *and palm leaf unmanufactured.*
NOTE.—New matter in italics.
565. Farina.
566. Fashion-plates, engraved on steel *or copper* or on wood, colored or plain.
NOTE.—New matter in italices.
567. Feathers and downs for beds.
Old law: Bed feathers and downs.
568. Feldspar.
569. Felt, adhesive, for sheathing vessels.
570. Fibrin, in all forms.
571. Fish, the product of American fisheries and fresh or frozen fish (except salmon) caught in fresh waters by American vessels, or with nets or other devices owned by citizens of the United States.
Old law: Fish, fresh, for immediate consumption.
572. Fish for bait.
573. Fish skins.
Also shark skins under old law.
574. Flint, flints, and ground flint stones.
575. Floor matting manufactured from round or split straw, including what is commonly known as Chinese matting.
Old law: Floor matting and floor mats exclusively of vegetable substances, twenty per centum.
576. Fossils.
577. Fruit-plants, tropical and semi-tropical, for the purpose of propagation or cultivation.
FRUITS AND NUTS—
578. Currants, Zante or other.
Old law: One cent per pound.
579. Dates.
Old law: One cent per pound.
580. Fruits, green, ripe, or dried, not specially provided for in this act.
581. Tamarinds.
582. Cocoa nuts.

583. Brazil nuts.
584. Cream nuts.
585. Palm nuts.
586. Palm-nut kernels.
587. Furs, undressed.
589. Fur-skins of all kinds not dressed in any manner.
589. Gambier.
590. Glass, broken, and old glass, which can not be cut for use, and fit only to be remanufactured.
591. Glass plates or disks, rough-cut or unwrought, for use in the manufacture of optical instruments, spectacles, and eye-glasses, and suitable only for such use: *Provided, however,* That such disks exceeding eight inches in diameter may be polished sufficiently to enable the character of the glass to be determined.

> Old law: Glass plates or disks, unwrought, for use in the manufacture of optical instruments.

GRASSES AND FIBERS—

592. Istle or Tampico fiber.
593. Jute.

> Old law: Twenty per centum.

594. Jute butts.

> Old law: Five dollars per ton.

595. Manilla.
596. Sisal-grass.

> Old law: Fifteen dollars per ton.

597. Sunn.

> Old law: Fifteen dollars per ton.

And all other textile grasses or fibrous vegetable substances, unmanufactured or undressed, not specially provided for in this act.

> Old law: Fifteen dollars per ton. Esparto or Spanish grass and other grasses, and pulp of, for the manufacture of paper.

598. Gold beaters' molds and gold beaters' skins.
599. Grease, and oils, such as are commonly used in soap-making or in wire-drawing, or for stuffing or dressing leather and which are fit only for such uses, not specially provided for in this act.

> Old law: Grease for use as soap stock only, not specially provided for; soap stocks free; grease, all not specially enumerated or provided for, ten per centum.

600. Guano, manures, and all substances expressly used for manure.
601. Gunny bags and gunny cloths, old or refuse, fit only for re-manufacture.
602. Guts, salted.
603. Gutta percha, crude.
604. Hair of horse, cattle, and other animals, cleaned or uncleaned, drawn or undrawn, but unmanufactured, not specially provided for in this act; and human hair, raw, uncleaned, and not drawn.

> Old law: Hair, horse or cattle, and hair of all kinds, cleaned or uncleaned, drawn or undrawn, but unmanufactured, not specially enumerated or provided for in this act: of hogs, curled for beds and mattresses, and not fit for bristles.

605. Hides, raw or uncured, whether dry, salted, or pickled. Angora goat-skins, raw, without the wool, unmanufactured, asses'

skins, raw or unmanufactured, and skins, except sheep-skins with the wool on.

> Old law: Also goat-skins raw.

606. Hide-cuttings, raw, with or without hair, and all *other* glue-stock.

> NOTE.—New matter in italics.

607. Hide rope.
608. Hones and whetstones.
609. Hoofs, *unmanufactured.*

> NOTE.—New matter in italics.

610. Hop roots for cultivation.
611. Horns and parts of, unmanufactured, including horn strips and tips.
612. Ice.
613. India rubber, crude, and milk of, and old scrap or refuse India rubber which has been worn out by use and is fit only for remanufacture.
614. Indigo.

> Old law: Indigo and artificial indigo.

615. Iodine, crude.
616. Ipecac.
617. Iridium.
618. Ivory and vegetable ivory, *not sawed, cut or otherwise manufactured.*

> NOTE.—New matter in italics. Old law contained word *unmanufactured.*

619. Jalap.
620. Jet, unmanufactured.
621. Joss-stick, or Joss-light.
622. Junk, old.
623. Kelp.
624. Kieserite.
625. Kyanite, or cyanite, and kainite.
626. Lac-dye, crude, seed, button, stick, and shell.
627. Lac spirits.
628. Lactarine.
629. Lava, unmanufactured.
630. Leeches.
631. Lemon juice, lime juice, *and sour-orange juice.*

> NOTE.—New matter in italics.

632. Licorice-root, unground
633. Life-boats and life-saving apparatus specially imported by societies incorporated or established to encourage the saving of human life.
634. Lime, citrate of.
635. Lime, chloride of, or bleaching-powder.
636. Lithographic stones not engraved.
637. Litmus, prepared or not prepared.
638. Loadstones.
639. Madder and munjeet, or Indian madder, ground or prepared, and all extracts of.
640. Magnesite, or native mineral carbonate of magnesia.
641. Magnesium.
642. Magnets.

643. Manganese, oxide and ore of.
644. Manna.
645. Manuscripts.
646. Marrow, crude.
647. Marsh mallows.
648. Medals of gold, silver, or copper, *such as trophies or prizes.*

NOTE.—New matter in italics.

649. Meerschaum, crude or unmanufactured.

Old law says raw instead of unmanufactured.

650. Mineral waters, all not artificial.
651. Minerals, crude, or not advanced in value or condition by refining or grinding, or by other process of manufacture. not specially provided for in this act.
652. Models of inventions and of other improvements in the arts, including patterns for machinery, but no article shall be deemed a model or pattern which can be fitted for use otherwise.

Old law: Changed from improvement to pattern.

653. Moss, sea-weeds, and vegetable substances, crude or unmanufactured, not otherwise specially provided for in this act.

Old law: Moss, sea-weeds, and all other vegetable substances used for beds and mattresses.

654. Musk, crude, in natural pods.
655. Myrobolan.
656. Needles, hand-sewing. and darning.
657. Newspapers and periodicals; *but the "term periodicals" as herein used shall be understood to embrace only unbound or paper-covered publications, containing current literature of the day and issued regularly at stated periods, as weekly, monthly, or quarterly.*

NOTE.—New matter in italics.

658. Nux vomica..
659. Oakum.
660. Oil cake.
661. OILS: Almond, amber, crude and rectified ambergris, anise or anise-seed, aniline, aspic or spike lavender, bergamot, cajeput, caraway, cassia, cinnamon, cedrat, chamomile, citronella or lemon grass, civet, fennel, Jasmine or Jasimine, Juglandium, Juniper, lavender, lemon, limes, mace, neroli or orange flower, nut oil or oil of nuts not otherwise specially provided for in this act, orange oil, olive oil for manufacturing or mechanical purposes unfit for eating and not otherwise provided for in this act, ottar of roses. palm and cocoanut, rosemary or anthoss, sesame or sesamum-seed or bene, thyme, origanum red or white, valerian; and also spermaceti, whale, and other fish oils of American fisheries, and all other articles the produce of such fisheries.
662. Olives, green or prepared.
663. Opium, crude or unmanufactured, and not adulterated, containing nine per centum and over of morphia.
664. Orange and lemon peel, not preserved, candied, or otherwise prepared.
665. Orchil, or orchil liquid.
666. Orchids, lily of the valley, azaleas, palms, and other plants used for forcing under glass for cut flowers or decorative purposes.
667. Ores, of gold, silver, *and nickel, and nickel matte : Provided, That ores of nickel, and nickel matte, containing more than two per*

centum of copper, shall pay a duty of one-half of one cent per pound on the copper contained therein.

Old law: All forms of nickel fifteen cents per pound.

668. Osmium.

669. Palladium.

670. Paper stock, crude, of every description, including all grasses, fibers, rags (other than wool), waste, shavings, clippings, old paper, rope ends, waste rope, waste bagging, old or refuse gunny bags or gunny cloth, and poplar or other woods, fit only to be converted into paper.

> Old law: Leather, old scraps, enumerated. Sea-weed not specially provided for. Paper-stock, crude, of every description, including all grasses, fibers, rags of all kinds, other than wool, waste, shavings, clippings, old paper, rope-ends, waste rope, waste bagging, gunny-bags, gunny-cloth, old or refuse, to be used in making, and fit only to be converted into paper, and unfit for any other manufacture, and cotton waste, whether for paper-stock or other purposes. Rags of whatever material composed, and not specially provided for in this act, ten per centum. (See fibers and grasses.)

671. Paraffine.

672. Parchment and vellum.

673. Pearl, mother of, *not sawed, cut, polished, or otherwise manufactured.*

NOTE.—New matter in italics.

674. Peltries and other usual goods and effects of Indians passing or repassing the boundary line of the United States, under such regulations as the Secretary of the Treasury may prescribe: *Provided,* That this exemption shall not apply to goods in bales or other packages unusual among Indians.

675. Personal and household effects not merchandise of citizens of the United States dying in foreign countries.

676. Pewter and britannia metal, old, and fit only to be re-manufactured.

677. Philosophical and scientific apparatus, instruments and preparations; statuary, casts of marble, bronze, alabaster, or plaster of Paris; paintings, drawings, and etchings, specially imported in good faith for the use of any society or institution incorporated or established for religious, philosophical, educational, scientific, or literary purposes, or for encouragement of the fine arts, and not intended for sale.

678. Phosphates, crude or native.

Old law contains words: "For fertilizing purposes."

679. Plants, trees, shrubs, roots, seed-cane, and seeds, all of the foregoing imported by the Department of Agriculture or the United States Botanic Garden.

680. Plaster of Paris and sulphate of lime, unground.

681. Platina, in ingots, bars, sheets, and wire.

Old law: Platina unmanufactured.

682. Platinum, unmanufactured, and vases, retorts, and other apparatus, vessels, and parts thereof *composed of platinum* for chemical uses.

NOTE.—New matter in italics.

683. Plumbago.

684. Polishing-stones.

685. Potash, crude, carbonate of, or "black salts." Caustic potash, or hydrate of, not including refined in sticks or rolls. Nitrate of potash, or saltpeter, crude. Sulphate of potash, crude or refined. Chlorate of potash. Muriate of potash.

> Old law: Caustic, and so forth, twenty per centum; chlorate, three cents per pound; sulphate, twenty per centum; nitrate of, or saltpeter crude, one cent per pound.

686. Professional books, implements, instruments, and tools of trade, occupation, or employment, in the actual possession at the time of persons arriving in the United States; but this exemption shall not be construed to include machinery or other articles imported for use in any manufacturing establishment, or for any other person or persons, or for sale.

> Old law: Professional books only.

687. Pulu.

688. Pumice.

689. Quills, prepared or unprepared, *but not made up into complete articles.*

> NOTE.—New matter in italics.

690. Quinia, sulphate of, and all alkaloids or salts of cinchona-bark.

> Old law: Quinia, sulphate of, salts of, and cinchonidia.

691. Rags not otherwise specially provided for in this act.

> Old law: Rags of all kinds other than wool.

692. Regalia and gems, statues, statuary and specimens of sculpture where specially imported in good faith for the use of any society incorporated or established *solely* for *educational,* philosophical, literary, or religious purposes, or for the encouragement of fine arts, or for the use or by order of any college, academy, school, seminary of learning, or public library in the United States ; *but the term "regalia" as herein used shall be held to embrace only such insignia of rank or office or emblems, as may be worn upon the person or borne in the hand during public exercises of the society or institution, and shall not include articles of furniture or fixtures, or of regular wearing-apparel, not personal property of individuals.*

> NOTE.—New matter in italics.

693. Rennets, raw or prepared.

694. Saffron and safflower, and extract of, and saffron cake.

695. Sago, crude, and sago flour.

696. Salacine.

697. Sauer-krout.

698. Sausage skins.

699. Seeds; anise, canary, caraway, cardamon, coriander, cotton, cummin, fennel, fenugreek, hemp, hoarhound, mustard, rape, Saint John's bread or bene, sugar-beet, mangel wurzel, sorghum or sugar cane for seed, and all flower and grass seeds ; bulbs and bulbous roots, not edible; all the foregoing not specially provided for in this act.

> Old law: Bulbs and bulbous roots, not medicinal, not otherwise provided for, twenty per centum.

700. Selep, or saloup.

701. Shells of all kinds, not cut, ground, or otherwise manufactured.

> Old law : Shells of every description, not manufactured ; tortoise and other shells, unmanufactured, free.

94

702. Shotgun barrels, forged, rough bored.
Old law: Ten per centum.
703. Shrimps, and other shell fish.
704. Silk, raw, or as reeled from the cocoon, but not doubled, twisted, or advanced in manufacture in any way.
705. Silk cocoons and silk-waste.
706. Silk worm's eggs.
707. Skeletons and other preparations of anatomy.
708. Snails.
709. Soda, nitrate of, or cubic nitrate, and chlorate of.
710. Sodium.
711. Sparterre, *suitable* for making or ornamenting hats
Note : New matter in italics.
712. Specimens of natural history, botany, and mineralogy, when imported for cabinets or as objects of science, and not for sale.
Old law extended to *objects of taste.*

SPICES—
713. Cassia, cassia vera, and cassia buds, unground.
714. Cinnamon, and chips of, unground.
715. Cloves and clove stems, unground.
716. Ginger-root, unground *and not preserved or candied.*
New matter in italics.
717. Mace.
718. Nutmegs.
719. Pepper, black or white, unground.
720. Pimento, unground.
721. Spunk.
722. Spurs and stilts used in the manufacture of earthen, porcelain, and stone ware.
Old law was crockery instead of porcelain.
723. Stone and sand : Burr-stone in blocks, rough or manufactured, and not bound up into mill-stones ; cliff-stone, unmanufactured, pumice-stone, rotten-stone, and sand, crude or manufactured.
724. Storax, or styrax.
725. Strontia, oxide of, and protoxide of strontian, and strontianite, or mineral carbonite of strontia.
726. Sugars, all not above number sixteen Dutch standard in color, all tank bottoms, all sugar drainings and sugar sweepings, sirups of cane juice, melada, concentrated melada, and concrete and concentrated molasses, and molasses.
Old law : All sugars not above No. 13 Dutch standard in color shall pay duty on their polariscopic test as follows, viz :
All sugars not above No. 13 Dutch standard in color, all tank bottoms, sirups of cane-juice or of beet-juice, melada, concentrated melada, concrete and concentrated molasses, testing by the polariscope not above seventy-five degrees, shall pay a duty of one and forty-hundredths cent per pound, and for every additional degree or fraction of a degree shown by the polariscopic test, they shall pay four-hundredths of a cent per pound additional : [*a. Provided,* That concentrated melada, or concrete, shall hereafter be classed as sugar * * * and melada shall be known and defined as an article made in the process of sugar-making being the cane-juice boiled down to the sugar point and containing all the sugar and molasses resulting from the boiling process and without any process of purging or clarification, and any and all products of the sugar-cane imported in bags, mats, baskets or other than tight pack-

ages shall be considered sugar and dutiable as such. *And provided further.* That of the drawback on refined sugars exported allowed by section three thousand and nineteen of the Revised Statutes of the United States, only one per centum of the amount so allowed shall be retained by the United States. Act of March 3, 1875, sec. 3.]

Sugar, thirteen to sixteen Dutch standard, two and seventy-five one hundredths cents per pound.

Old law : Molasses testing not above fifty-six degrees by the polariscope, shall pay a duty of four cents per gallon ; molasses testing above fifty-six degrees, shall pay a duty of eight cents per gallon.

727. Sulphur, lac or precipitated, and sulphur or brimstone, crude, in bulk, sulphur ore, as pyrites, or sulphuret of iron in its natural state, containing in excess of twenty-five per centum of sulphur (except on the copper contained therein) and sulphur not otherwise provided for.

Old law : Sulphur, or brimstone, not specially enumerated or provided for in this act; sulphur, lac or precipitated, free.

728. Sulphuric acid which at the temperature of sixty degrees Fahrenheit does not exceed the specific gravity of one and three hundred and eighty thousandths, for use in manufacturing superphosphate of lime or artificial manures of any kind, or for any agricultural purposes.

Old law: Free under general provision for acid.

729. Sweepings of silver and gold.

730. Tapioca, cassava or cassady.

731. Tar and pitch of wood, and pitch of coal-tar.

Old law: Wood tar, ten per centum; coal tar, crude, ten per centum ad valorem.

732. Tea and tea-plants.

733. Teeth, *natural, or* unmanufactured.

New matter in italics.

734. Terra alba.

Word aluminous omitted.

735. Terra japonica.

736. Tin ore, cassiterite or black oxide of tin, and tin in bars, blocks, pigs, or grain or granulated, until July the first, eighteen hundred and ninety-three, and thereafter as otherwise provided for in this act.

737. Tinsel wire, lame, or lahn.

738. Tobacco stems.

Old law: Fifteen cents per pound.

739. Tonquin, tonqua, or tonka beans.

740. Tripoli.

741. Turmeric.

742. Turpentine, Venice.

743. Turpentine, spirits of

Old law: Twenty cents per gallon.

744. Turtles.

745. Types, old, and fit only to be remanufactured.

746. Uranium, oxide and salts of.

747. Vaccine virus.

748. Valonia.

749. Verdigris, or subacetate of copper

750. Wafers, unmedicated.

751. Wax, vegetable or mineral.

752. Wearing apparel and other personal effects (not merchandise) of persons arriving in the United States, but this exemption shall not be held to include articles not actually in use and necessary and appropriate for the use of such persons for the purposes of their journey and present comfort and convenience, or which are intended for any other person or persons, or for sale: *Provided, however,* That all such wearing apparel and other personal effects as may have been - once imported into the United States and subjected to the payment of duty, and which may have been actually used and taken or exported to foreign countries by the persons returning therewith to the United States, shall, if not advanced in value or improved in condition by any means since their exportation from the United States, be entitled to exemption from duty, upon their identity being established, under such rules and regulations as may be prescribed by the Secretary of the Treasury.

> Old law: Wearing apparel, in actual use, and other personal effects (not merchandise), professional books, implements, instruments, and tools of trade, occupation, or employment of persons arriving in the United States. But this exemption shall not be construed to include machinery or other articles imported for use in any manufacturing establishment, or for sale.

753. Whalebone, unmanufactured.

754. Wood.—Logs, and round unmanufactured timber not specially enumerated or provided for in this act.

755. Fire wood, handle-bolts, heading-bolts, stave-bolts, shingle-bolts, hop-poles, fence-posts, railroad ties, ship timber, and ship-planking, not specially provided for in this act.

756. Woods, namely, cedar, lignum-vitæ, lancewood, ebony, box, granadilla, mahogany, rosewood, satinwood, and all *forms of* cabinet-woods, in the log, rough or hewn; bamboo and rattan unmanufactured; briar-root or briar-wood, and similar wood unmanufactured, or not further manufactured than cut into blocks suitable for the articles into which they are intended to be converted; bamboo, reeds, and sticks of partridge, hair-wood, pimento, orange, myrtle, and other woods not otherwise specially provided for in this act, in the rough, or not further manufactured than cut into lengths suitable for sticks for umbrellas, parasols, sun-shades, whips, or walking-canes; and India malacca joints, not further manufactured than cut into suitable lengths for the manufactures into which they are intended to be converted.

New matter in italics.

757. Works of art, the production of American artists residing temporarily abroad, or other works of art, including pictorial paintings on glass, imported expressly for presentation to a national institution, or to any State or municipal corporation, or incorporated religious society, college, or other public institution, except stained or painted window-glass or stained or painted glass windows; but such exemption shall be subject to such regulations as the Secretary of the Treasury may prescribe.

> Old law: Works of art, painting, statuary, fountains, and other works of art, the production of American artists. But the fact of such production must be verified by the certificate of a consul or minister of the United States indorsed upon the written declaration of the artist; paintings, statuary, fountains, and other works of art, imported expressly for presentation to national institutions, or to any State, or to any municipal corporation, or religious corporation or society.

758. Works of art, drawings, engravings, photographic pictures, and philosophical and scientific apparatus brought by professional artists, lecturers, or scientists arriving from abroad for use by them temporarily for exhibition and in illustration, promotion, and encouragement of art, science, or industry in the United States, and not for sale, and photographic pictures, paintings, and statuary, imported for exhibition by any association established in good faith and duly authorized under the laws of the United States, or of any State, expressly and solely for the promotion and encouragement of science, art, or industry, and not intended for sale, shall be admitted free of duty, under such regulations as the Secretary of the Treasury shall prescribe; but bonds shall be given for the payment to the United States of such duties as may be imposed by law upon any and all of such articles as shall not be exported within six months after such importation: *Provided,* That the Secretary of the Treasury may, in his discretion, extend such period for a further term of six months in cases where applications therefor shall be made.

759. Works of art, collections in illustration of the progress of the arts, science, or manufactures, photographs, works in terra-cotta, parian, pottery, or porcelain, and artistic copies of antiquities in metal or other material hereafter imported in good faith for permanent exhibition at a fixed place by any society or institution established for the encouragement of the arts or of science, and all like articles imported in good faith by any society or association for the purpose of erecting a public monument, and not intended for sale, nor for any other purpose than herein expressed; but bonds shall be given under such rules and regulations as the Secretary of the Treasury may prescribe, for the payment of lawful duties which may accrue should any of the articles aforesaid be sold, transferred, or used contrary to this provision, and such articles shall be subject, at any time, to examination and inspection by the proper officers of the customs: *Provided.* That the privileges of this and the preceding section shall not be allowed to associations or corporations engaged in or connected with business of a private or commercial character.

760. Yams.

761. Zaffer.

SEC. 3. That with a view to secure reciprocal trade with countries producing the following articles, and for this purpose, on and after the first day of January eighteen hundred and ninety-two, whenever, and so often as the President shall be satisfied that the Government of any country producing and exporting sugars, molasses, coffee, tea, and hides, raw and uncured, or any of such articles, imposes duties or other exactions upon the agricultural or other products of the United States, which in view of the free introduction of such sugar, molasses, coffee, tea, and hides into the United States he may deem to be reciprocally unequal and unreasonable, he shall have the power and it shall be his duty to suspend, by proclamation to that effect, the provisions of this act relating to the free introduction of such sugar, molasses, coffee, tea, and hides, the production of such country, for such time as he shall deem just, and in such case and during such suspension duties shall be levied, collected, and paid upon sugar, molasses, coffee, tea, and hides, the product of or exported from such designated country as follows, namely:

All sugars not above number thirteen Dutch standard in color shall pay duty on their polariscopic tests as follows, namely:

All sugars not above number thirteen Dutch standard in color, all tank bottoms, sirups of cane juice or of beet juice, melada, concentrated melada, concrete and concentrated molasses, testing by the polariscope not above seventy-five degrees, seven-tenths of one cent per pound; and for every additional degree or fraction of a degree shown by the polariscopic test, two hundredths of one cent per pound additional.

All sugars above number thirteen Dutch standard in color shall be classified by the Dutch standard of color, and pay duty as follows, namely: All sugar above number thirteen and not above number sixteen Dutch standard of color, one and three-eighths cents per pound.

All sugar above number sixteen and not above number twenty Dutch standard of color, one and five-eighths cents per pound.

All sugars above number twenty Dutch standard of color, two cents per pound.

Molasses testing above fifty-six degrees, four cents per gallon.

Sugar drainings and sugar sweepings shall be subject to duty either as molasses or sugar, as the case may be, according to polariscopic test.

On coffee, three cents per pound.

On tea, ten cents per pound.

Hides, raw or uncured, whether dry, salted, or pickled, Angora goat-skins, raw, without the wool, unmanufactured, asses' skins, raw or unmanufactured, and skins, except sheep-skins, with the wool on, one and one-half cents per pound.

Section three is new matter.

Sec. 4. That there shall be levied, collected, and paid on the importation of all raw or unmanufactured articles, not enumerated or provided for in this act, a duty of ten per centum ad valorem; and on all articles manufactured, in whole or in part, not provided for in this act, a duty of twenty per centum ad valorem.

Old law: Ammonia, aqua or water of, twenty per centum.
Ammonia, anhydrous, liquefied by pressure, twenty per centum.
Coal-tar, products of, such as naphtha, benzine, benzole, dead oil, and pitch, twenty per centum ad valorem.
All non-dutiable crude minerals, but which have been advanced in value or condition by refining or grinding, or by other process of manufacture, not specially enumerated or provided for in this act, ten per centum.
Candles and tapers of all kinds, twenty per centum.

Sec. 5. That each and every imported article, not enumerated in this act, which is similar, either in material, quality, texture, or the use to which it may be applied, to any article enumerated in this act as chargeable with duty shall pay the same rate of duty which is levied on the enumerated article which it most resembles in any of the particulars before mentioned; and if any non-enumerated article equally resembles two or more enumerated articles on which different rates of duty are chargeable there shall be levied on such non-enumerated article the same rate of duty as is chargeable on the article which it resembles paying the highest rate of duty; and on articles not enumerated, manufactured of two or more materials, the duty shall be assessed at the highest rate at which the same would be chargeable if composed wholly of the component material thereof of chief value; and the words "component material of chief value," wherever used in this act, shall be held to mean that component material which shall exceed in value any other single component material of the article; and the value of each component material shall be determined by the ascertained value of such material in its condition as found in the article. If two or more rates of duty shall be applicable to any imported article it shall pay duty at the highest of such rates.

Old law: SEC. 2499. There shall be levied, collected, and paid on each and every non-enumerated article which bears a similitude, either in material, quality, texture, or the use to which it may be applied, to any article enumerated in this title as chargeable with duty, the same rate of duty which is levied and charged on the enumerated article which it most resembles in any of the particulars before mentioned; and if any non-enumerated article equally resembles two or more enumerated articles on which different rates are chargeable, there shall be levied, collected, and paid on such non-enumerated article the same rate of duty as is chargeable on the article which it resembles paying the highest duty; and on all articles manufactured from two or more materials the duty shall be assessed at the highest rates at which the component material of chief value may be chargeable. If two or more rates of duty should be applicable to any imported article, it shall be classified for duty under the highest of such rates: *Provided*, That non-enumerated articles similar in material and quality and texture, and the use to which they may be applied, to articles on the free list, and in the manufacture of which no dutiable materials are used, shall be free.

SEC. 6. That on and after the first day of March, eighteen hundred and ninety-one, all articles of foreign manufacture, such as are usually or ordinarily marked, stamped, branded, or labeled, and all packages containing such or other imported articles, shall, respectively, be plainly marked, stamped, branded, or labeled in legible English words, so as to indicate the country of their origin; and unless so marked, stamped, branded, or labeled they shall not be admitted to entry.

Section six is new matter.

SEC. 7. That on and after March first, eighteen hundred and ninety-one, no article of imported merchandise which shall copy or simulate the name or trade-mark of any domestic manufacture or manufacturer, shall be admitted to entry at any custom-house of the United States. And in order to aid the officers of the customs in enforcing this prohibition any domestic manufacturer who has adopted trade-marks may require his name and residence and a description of his trade-marks to be recorded in books which shall be kept for that purpose in the Department of the Treasury under such regulations as the Secretary of the Treasury shall prescribe, and may furnish to the Department fac-similes of such trade-marks; and thereupon the Secretary of the Treasury shall cause one or more copies of the same to be transmitted to each collector or other proper officer of the customs.

Old law: SEC. 2496. No watches, watch-cases, watch-movements, or parts of watch movements, or any other articles of foreign manufacture, which shall copy or simulate the name or trade-mark of any domestic manufacture, [manufacturer,] shall be admitted to entry at the custom-house of the United States, unless such domestic manufacturer is the importer of the same. And in order to aid the officers of the customs in enforcing this prohibition, any domestic manufacturer who has adopted trade-marks may require his name and residence and a description of his trade-marks to be recorded in books which shall be kept for that purpose in the Department of the Treasury, under such regulations as the Secretary of the Treasury shall prescribe, and may furnish to the department fac similes of such trade-marks; and thereupon the Secretary of the Treasury shall cause one or more copies of the same to be transmitted to each collector or other proper officer of the customs.

SEC. 8. That all lumber, timber, hemp, manilla, *wire rope*, and iron and steel rods, bars, spikes, nails, *plates, tees, angles, beams*, and bolts and copper and composition metal which may be necessary for the construction and equipment of vessels built in the United States *for foreign account and ownership or* for the purpose of being employed in the foreign trade, including the trade between the Atlantic and Pacific ports of the United States, after the passage of this act, may be imported in bond, under such regulations as the Secretary of the Treasury may prescribe ; and upon proof that such materials have been used for such purpose no duties shall be paid thereon. But vessels receiving the benefit of this section shall not be allowed to engage in the coastwise trade of the United States more than two months in any one year, except upon the payment to the United States of the duties on which a rebate is herein allowed : *Provided, That vessels built in the United States for foreign account and ownership shall not be allowed to engage in the coastwise trade of the United States.*

NOTE.—New matter in italics.

SEC. 9. That all articles of foreign production needed for the repair of American vessels engaged in foreign trade, *including the trade between the Atlantic and Pacific ports of the United States*, may be withdrawn from bonded-warehouses free of duty, under such regulations as the Secretary of the Treasury may prescribe.

NOTE.—New matter in italics.

SEC. 10. That all medicines, preparations, compositions, perfumery, cosmetics, cordials, and other liquors manufactured wholly or in part of domestic spirits, intended for exportation, as provided by law, in order to be manufactured and sold or removed, without being charged with duty and without having a stamp affixed thereto, shall, under such regulations as the Secretary of the Treasury may prescribe, be made and manufactured in warehouses similarly constructed to those known and designated in Treasury regulations as bonded-warehouses, class two : *Provided*, That such manufacturer shall first give satisfactory bonds to the collector of internal revenue for the faithful observance of all the provisions of law and the regulations as aforesaid, in amount not less than half of that required by the regulations of the Secretary of the Treasury from persons allowed bonded-warehouses. Such goods, when manufactured in such warehouses, may be removed for exportation under the direction of the proper officer having charge thereof, who shall be designated by the Secretary of the Treasury without being charged with duty, and without having a stamp affixed thereto. Any manufacturer of the articles aforesaid, or any of them, having such bonded warehouse as aforesaid, shall be at liberty, under such regulations as the Secretary of the Treasury may prescribe, to convey therein any materials to be used in such manufacture which are allowed by the provisions of law to be exported free from tax or duty, as well as the necessary materials, implements, packages, vessels, brands, and labels for the preparation, putting up, and export of the said manufactured articles; and every article so used shall be exempt from the payment of stamp and excise duty by such manufacturer. Articles and materials so to be used may be transferred from any bonded-warehouse in which the same may be, under such regulation as the Secretary of the Treasury may prescribe, into any bonded-warehouse in which such manufacture may be conducted, and may be used in such manufacture, and when so used shall be exempt from stamp and excise duty; and the receipt of the officer in charge as aforesaid shall be received as a voucher for the manufacture of such articles. Any materials imported into the United States may, under such rules as the Secretary of the Treasury may prescribe, and under the direction of the proper officer, be removed in original packages from on shipboard, or from the bonded-warehouse in which the same may be, into the bonded-warehouse in which such manufacture may be carried on, for the purpose of being used in such manufacture, without payment of duties thereon, and may there be used in such manufacture. No article so removed, nor any article manufactured in said bonded-warehouse, shall be taken therefrom except for exportation, under the direction of the proper officer having charge thereof as aforesaid, whose certificate, describing the articles by their mark or otherwise, the quantity, the date of importation, and name of vessel, with such additional particulars as may from time to time be required, shall be received by the collector of customs in cancellation of the bond or return of the amount of foreign import duties. All labor performed and services rendered under these regulations shall be under the supervision of an officer of the customs, and at the expense of the manufacturer.

Some change in text.

Sec. 11. All persons are prohibited from importing into the United States from any foreign country any obscene book, pamphlet, paper, writing, advertisement, circular, print, picture, drawing, or other representation, figure, or image on or of paper or other material, or any cast, instrument, or other article of an immoral nature, or any drug or medicine, or any article whatever, for the prevention of conception, or for causing unlawful abortion. No such articles, whether imported separately or contained in packages with other goods entitled to entry, shall be admitted to entry; and all such articles shall be proceeded against, seized, and forfeited by due course of law. All such prohibited articles and the package in which they are contained in the course of importation shall be detained by the officer of customs, and proceedings taken against the same as prescribed in the following section, unless it appears to the satisfaction of the collector of customs that the obscene articles contained in the package were inclosed therein without the knowledge or consent of the importer, owner, agent, or consignee: *Provided*, That the drugs hereinbefore mentioned, when imported in bulk and not put up for any of the purposes hereinbefore specified, are excepted from the operation of this section.

Note.—Changes text of sections 2491, 2492, 2493, Revised Statutes.

Sec 12. That whoever, being an officer, agent, or employee of the Government of the United States, shall knowingly aid or abet any person engaged in any violation of any of the provisions of law prohibiting importing, advertising, dealing in, exhibiting, or sending or receiving by mail obscene or indecent publications or representations, or means for preventing conception or procuring abortion, or other articles of indecent or immoral use or tendency, shall be deemed guilty of a misdemeanor, and shall for every offense be punishable by a fine of not more than five thousand dollars, or by imprisonment at hard labor for not more than ten years, or both.

SEC. 13. That any judge of any district or circuit court of the United States, within the proper district, before whom complaint in writing of any violation of the two preceding sections is made, to the satisfaction of such judge, and founded on knowledge or belief, and if upon belief, setting forth the grounds of such belief, and supported by oath or affirmation of the complainant may issue, conformably to the Constitution, a warrant directed to the marshal or any deputy marshal, in the proper district, directing him to search for, seize, and take possession of any such article or thing mentioned in the two preceding sections, and to make due and immediate return thereof to the end that the same may be condemned and destroyed by proceedings, which shall be conducted in the same manner as other proceedings in the case of municipal seizure, and with the same right of appeal or writ of error.

SEC. 14. That machinery for repair may be imported into the United States without payment of duty, under bond, to be given in double the appraised value thereof, to be withdrawn and exported after said machinery shall have been repaired; and the Secretary of the Treasury is authorized and directed to prescribe such rules and regulations as may be necessary to protect the revenue against fraud, and secure the identity and character of all such importations when again withdrawn and exported, restricting and limiting the export and withdrawal to the same port of entry where imported, and also limiting all bonds to a period of time of not more than six months from the date of the importation.

SEC. 15. That the produce of the forests of the State of Maine upon the Saint John River and its tributaries, owned by American citizens, and sawed or hewed in the Province of New Brunswick by American citizens, the same being unmanufactured in whole or in part, which is now admitted into the ports of the United States free of duty, shall continue to be so admitted under such regulations as' the Secretary of the Treasury shall, from time to time, prescribe.

SEC. 16. That the produce of the forests of the State of Maine upon the Saint Croix River and its tributaries owned by American citizens, and sawed in the Province of New Brunswick by American citizens, the same being unmanufactured in whole or in part, shall be admitted into the ports of the United States free of duty, under such regulations as the Secretary of the Treasury shall, from time to time, prescribe.

SEC. 17. That a discriminating duty of ten per centum ad valorem, in addition to the duties imposed by law, shall be levied, collected, and paid on all goods, wares, or merchandise which shall be imported in vessels not of the United States; but this discriminating duty shall not apply to goods, wares, and merchandise which shall be imported in vessels not of the United States, entitled, by treaty or any act of Congress, to be entered in the ports of the United States on payment of the same duties as shall then be paid on goods, wares, and merchandise imported in vessels of the United States.

SEC. 18. That no goods, wares, or merchandise, unless in cases provided for by treaty, shall be imported into the United States from any foreign port or place, except in vessels of the United States, or in such foreign vessels as truly and wholly belong to the citizens or subjects of that country of which the goods are the growth, production, or manufacture, or from which such goods, wares, or merchandise can only be, or most usually are, first shipped for transportation. All goods, wares, or merchandise imported contrary to this section, and the vessel wherein the same shall be imported, together with her cargo, tackle, apparel, and furniture, shall be forfeited to the United States; and such goods, wares, or merchandise, ship, or vessel, and cargo shall be liable to be seized, prosecuted, and condemned, in like manner, and under the same regulations, restrictions, and provisions as have been heretofore established for the recovery, collection, distribution, and remission of forfeitures to the United States by the several revenue laws.

SEC. 19. That the preceding section shall not apply to vessels or goods, wares, or merchandise imported in vessels of a foreign nation which does not maintain a similar regulation against vessels of the United States.

SEC. 20. That the importation of neat cattle and the hides of neat cattle from any foreign country into the United States is prohibited : *Provided*, That the operation of this section shall be suspended as to any foreign country or countries, or any parts of such country or countries, whenever the Secretary of the Treasury shall officially determine, and give public notice thereof that such importation will not tend to the introduction or spread of contagious or infectious diseases among the cattle of the United States: and the Secretary of the Treasury is hereby authorized and empowered, and it shall be his duty, to make all necessary orders and regulations to carry this section into effect, or to suspend the same as therein provided, and to send copies thereof to the proper officers in the United States, and to such officers or agents of the United States in foreign Countries as he shall judge necessary.

SEC. 21. That any person convicted of a willful violation of any of the provisions of the preceding section shall be fined not exceeding five hundred dollars, or imprisoned not exceeding one year, or both, in the discretion of the Court.

SEC. 22. That upon the reimportation of articles once exported of the growth, product, or manufacture of the United States, upon which no internal tax has been assessed or paid, or upon which such tax has been paid and refunded by allowance or drawback, there shall be levied, collected, and paid a duty equal to the tax imposed by the internal-revenue laws upon such articles, *except articles manufactured in bonded warehouses and exported pursuant to law, which shall be subject to the same rate of duty as if originally imported.*

NOTE.—Text in italics represents new matter.

SEC. 23. That whenever any vessel laden with merchandise in whole or in part subject to duty has been sunk in any river, harbor, bay, or water subject to the jurisdiction of the United States, and within its limits, for the period of two years, and is abandoned by the owner thereof, any person who may raise such vessel shall be permitted to bring any merchandise recovered therefrom into the port nearest to the place where such vessel was so raised, free from the payment of any duty thereupon, and without being obliged to enter the same at the custom-house; but under such regulations as the Secretary of the Treasury may prescribe.

SEC. 24. That the works of manufactures engaged in smelting or refining metals in the United States may be designated as bonded-warehouses under such regulations as the Secretary of the Treasury may prescribe: *Provided*, That such manufacturers shall first give satisfactory bonds to the Secretary of Treasury. Metals in any crude form requiring smelting or refining to make them readily available in the arts, imported into the United States to be smelted or refined and intended to be exported in a refined but unmanufactured state, shall, under such rules as the Secretary of the Treasury may prescribe and under the direction of the proper officer, be removed in original packages or in bulk from the vessel or other vehicle on which it has been imported, or from the bonded-warehouse in which the same may be into the bonded-warehouse in which such smelting and refining may be carried on, for the purpose of being smelted and refined without payment of duties thereon, and may there be smelted and refined, together with other metals of home or foreign production: *Provided*, That each day a quantity of refined metal equal to the amount of imported metal refined that day shall be set aside, and such metal so set aside shall not be taken from said works except for exportation, under the direction of the proper officer having charge thereof as aforesaid, whose certificate, describing the articles by their marks or otherwise, the quantity, the date of importation, and the name of vessel or other vehicle by which it was imported, with such additional particulars as may from time to time be required, shall be received by the collector of customs as sufficient evidence of the exportation of the metal, or it may be removed, under such regulations as the Secretary of the Treasury may prescribe, to any other bonded-warehouse, or upon entry for, and payment of duties, for domestic consumption. All labor performed and services rendered under these regulations shall be under the supervision of an officer of the customs, to be appointed by the Secretary of the Treasury, and at the expense of the manufacturer.

Note.—New provision.

Sec. 25. That where imported materials on which duties have been paid, are used in the manufacture of articles manufactured or produced in the United States, there shall be allowed on the exportation of such articles a drawback equal in amount to the duties paid on the materials used, less one per centum of such duties: *Provided*, That when the articles exported are made in part from domestic materials, the imported materials, or the parts of the articles made from such materials shall so appear in the completed articles that the quantity or measure thereof may be ascertained. *And provided further*, That the drawback on any article allowed under existing law shall be continued at the rate herein provided. That the imported materials used in the manufacture or production of articles entitled to drawback of customs duties when exported shall in all cases where drawback of duties paid on such materials is claimed, be identified, the quantity of such materials used and the amount of duties paid thereon shall be ascertained, the facts of the manufacture or production of such articles in the United States and their exportation therefrom shall be determined, and the drawback due thereon shall be paid to the manufacturer, producer, or exporter, to the agent of either or to the person to whom such manufacturer, producer, exporter or agent shall in writing order such drawback paid, under such regulations as the Secretary of the Treasury shall prescribe.

This is an enlargement of the provisions of sections 3019 and 3020 Revised Statutes.

SEC. 26. That on and after the first day of May, eighteen hundred and ninety-one, all special taxes imposed by the laws now in force upon dealers in leaf tobacco, retail dealers in leaf tobacco, dealers in tobacco, manufacturers of tobacco, manufacturers of cigars, and peddlers of tobacco are here by repealed. Every such dealer in leaf tobacco, retail dealer in leaf tobacco, manufacturer, and peddler shall, however, register with the collector of the district his name, or style, place of residence, trade, or business, and the place where such trade or business is to be carried on, the same as though the tax had not been repealed, and a failure to register as herein required shall subject such person to a penalty of fifty dollars.

New matter.

SEC. 27. That all provisions of the statutes imposing restrictions of any kind whatsoever upon farmers and growers of tobacco in regard to the sale of their leaf tobacco, and the keeping of books, and the registration and report of their sales of leaf tobacco, or imposing any tax on account of such sales, are hereby repealed: *Provided, however,* That it shall be the duty of every farmer or planter producing and selling leaf-tobacco, on demand of any internal-revenue officer, or other authorized agent of the Treasury Department, to furnish said officer or agent a true and complete statement, verified by oath, of all his sales of leaf-tobacco, the number of hogsheads, cases, or pounds, with the name and residence, in each instance, of the person to whom sold, and the place to which it is shipped. And every farmer or planter who willfully refuses to furnish such information, or who knowingly makes false statements as to any of the facts aforsaid, shall be guilty of a misdemeanor, and shall be liable to a penalty not exceeding five hundred dollars.

New matter.

SEC. 28. That section thirty-three hundred and eighty-one of the Revised Statutes, be, and the same is hereby, amended by striking out all after the said number and substituting therefor the following:

"Every peddler of tobacco, before commencing, or, if he has already commenced, before continuing to peddle tobacco, shall furnish to the collector of his district a statement accurately setting forth the place of his residence, and, if in a city the street and number of the street where he resides, the State or States through which he proposes to travel; also whether he proposes to sell his own manufactures or the manufactures of others, and, if he sells for other parties, the person for whom he sells. He shall also give a bond in the sum of five hundred dollars, to be approved by the collector of the district, conditioned that he shall not engage in any attempt, by himself or by collusion with others, to defraud the Government of any tax on tobacco, snuff, or cigars; that he shall neither sell nor offer for sale any tobacco, snuff, or cigars, except in original and full packages, as the law requires the same to be put up and prepared by the manufacturer for sale, or for removal for sale or consumption, and except such packages of tobacco, snuff, and cigars as bear the manufacturer's label or caution notice, and his legal marks and brands, and genuine internal-revenue stamps which have never before been used."

SEC. 29. That section thirty-three hundred and eighty-three, Revised Statutes, as amended by section fifteen of the act of March first, eighteen hundred and seventy-nine, be, and the same is hereby, amended by striking out all of said section and by substituting in lieu thereof the following:

"Every peddler of tobacco shall obtain a certificate from the collector of his collection district, who is hereby authorized and directed to issue the same, giving the name of the peddler, his residence, and the fact of his having filed the required bond; and shall on demand of any officer of internal revenue produce and exhibit his certificate. And whenever any peddler refuses to exhibit his certificate, as aforesaid, on demand of any officer of internal revenue, said officer may seize the horse or mule, wagon, and contents, or pack, bundle, or basket, of any person so refusing; and the collector of the district in which the seizure occurs may, on ten days' notice, published in any newspaper in the district, or served personally on the peddler, or at his dwelling house, require such peddler to show cause, if any he has, why the horses or mules, wagons, and contents, pack, bundle, or basket so seized shall not be forfeited. In case no sufficient cause is shown, proceedings for the forfeiture of the property seized shall be taken under the general provisions of the internal-revenue laws relating to forfeitures. Any internal-revenue agent may demand production of and inspect the collector's certificate for peddlers, and refusal or failure to produce the same, when so demanded, shall subject the party guilty thereof to a fine of not more than five hundred dollars and to imprisonment for not more than twelve months."

SEC. 30. That on and after the first day of January, eighteen hundred and ninety-one, the internal taxes on smoking and manufactured tobacco shall be six cents per pound, and on snuff six cents per pound.

Old law: Eight cents per pound.

SEC. 31. That section thirty-three hundred and sixty-three, of the Revised Statutes, be, and hereby is, amended by striking out all after said number and substituting the following:

"No manufactured tobacco shall be sold or offered for sale unless put up in packages and stamped as prescribed in this chapter, except at retail by retail dealers from packages authorized by section thirty-three hundred and sixty-two of the Revised Statutes; and every person who sells or offers for sale any snuff or any kind of manufactured tobacco not so put up in packages and stamped shall be fined not not less than five hundred dollars nor more than five thousand dollars, and imprisoned not less than six months nor more than two years."

SEC. 32. That section thirty-three hundred and ninety-two of the Revised Statutes, as amended by section sixteen of the act of March first, eighteen hundred and seventy-nine, be and the same hereby is amended to read as follows:

"All cigars shall be packed in boxes not before used for that purpose, containing respectively twenty-five, fifty, one hundred, two hundred, two hundred and fifty, or five hundred cigars each: *Provided, however,* That manufacturers of cigars shall be permitted to pack in boxes not before used for that purpose cigars not to exceed thirteen nor less than twelve in number, to be used as sample boxes; and every person who sells, or offers for sale, or delivers, or offers to deliver, any cigars in any other form than in new boxes as above described, or who packs in any box any cigars in excess of or less than the number provided by law to be put in each box respectively, or who falsely brands any box, or affixes a stamp on any box denoting a less amount of tax than that required by law, shall be fined for each offense not more than one thousand dollars, and be imprisoned not more than two years: *Provided*, That nothing in this section shall be construed as preventing the sale of cigars at retail by retail dealers who have paid the special tax as such from boxes packed, stamped, and branded in the manner prescribed by law: *And provided further*, That every manufacturer of cigarettes shall put up all the cigarettes that he manufactures or has manufactured for him, and sells or removes for consumption or use, in packages or parcels containing ten, twenty, fifty, or one hundred cigarettes each, and shall securely affix to each of said packages or parcels a suitable stamp denoting the tax thereon, and shall properly cancel the same prior to such sale or removal for consumption or use, under such regulations as the Commissioner of Internal Revenue shall prescribe; and all cigarettes imported from a foreign country shall be packed, stamped, and the stamps canceled in like manner, in addition to the import stamp indicating inspection of the custom-house before they are withdrawn therefrom.

SEC. 33. That section thirty-three hundred and fifty-seven, of the Revised Statutes, as amended by section two of the act of June ninth, eighteen hundred and eighty, be, and the same is amended, by striking out all after the number and inserting in lieu thereof the following:

"Every collector shall keep a record, in a book or books provided for that purpose, to be open to the inspection of only the proper officers of internal revenue, including deputy collectors and internal-revenue agents, of the name and residence of every person engaged in the manufacture of tobacco or snuff in his district, the place where such manufacture is carried on, and the number of the manufactory; and he shall enter in said record, under the name of each manufacturer, a copy of every inventory required by law to be made by such manufacturer, and an abstract of his monthly returns; and he shall cause the several manufactories of tobacco or snuff in his district to be numbered consecutively, which numbers shall not be thereafter changed, except for reasons satisfactory to himself and approved by the Commissioner of Internal Revenue."

SEC. 34. That section thirty-three hundred and eighty-nine of the Revised Statutes, as amended by section sixteen of the act of March first, eighteen hundred and seventy-nine, be, and the same is hereby amended so as to read as follows:

"Every collector shall keep a record, in a book provided for that purpose, to be open to the inspection of only the proper officers of internal revenue, including deputy collectors and internal-revenue agents, of the name and residence of every person engaged in the manufacture of cigars in his district, the place where such manufacture is carried on, and the number of the manufactory; and he shall enter in said record, under the name of each manufacturer an abstract of his inventory and monthly returns; and he shall cause the several manufacturers of cigars in the district to be numbered consecutively, which number shall not thereafter be changed."

SEC. 35. That section three thousand three hundred and eighty-seven of the Revised Statutes, as amended by section sixteen of the act of March first, one thousand eight hundred and seventy-nine, be, and the same is hereby, amended by striking from the said section the following words, namely: "five hundred dollars, with an additional one hundred dollars for each person proposed to be employed by him in making cigars," and inserting in lieu of the words so stricken out the words: "one hundred dollars."

SEC. 36. That an internal-revenue tax of ten dollars per pound shall be levied and collected upon all opium manufactured in the United States for smoking purposes; and no person shall engage in such manufacture who is not a citizen of the United States and who has not given the bond required by the Commissioner of Internal Revenue

New matter.

• SEC. 37. That every manufacturer of such opium shall file with the collector of internal revenue of the district in which his manufactory is located such notices, inventories, and bonds, shall keep such books and render such returns of material and products, shall put up such signs and affix such number to his factory, and conduct his business under such surveillance of officers and agents as the Commissioner of Internal Revenue, with the approval of the Secretary of the Treasury, may, by regulation, require. But the bond required of such manufacturer shall be with sureties satisfactory to the collector of internal revenue and in a penal sum of not less than five thousand dollars; and the sum of said bond may be increased from time to time and additional sureties required at the discretion of the collector or under instructions of the Commissioner of Internal Revenue.

New matter.

SEC. 38. That all prepared smoking opium imported into the United States shall, before removal from the custom-house, be duly stamped in such manner as to denote that the duty thereon has been paid; and that all opium manufactured in the United States for smoking purposes, before being removed from the place of manufacture, whether for consumption or storage, shall be duly stamped in such permanent manner as to denote the payment of the internal-revenue tax thereon.

SEC. 39. That the provisions of existing laws governing the engraving, issue, sale, accountability, effacement, cancellation, and destruction of stamps relating to tobacco and snuff, as far as applicable are hereby made to apply to stamps provided for by the preceding section.

New matter.

SEC. 40. That a penalty of not more than one thousand dollars, or imprisonment not more than one year, or both, in the discretion of the court shall be imposed for each and every violation of the preceding sections of this act relating to opium by any person or persons; and all prepared smoking opium wherever found within the United States without stamps required by this act shall be forfeited.

New matter.

SEC. 41. That wholesale dealers in oleomargarine shall keep such books and render such returns in relation thereto as the Commissioner of Internal Revenue, with the approval of the Secretary of the Treasury, may, by regulation, require, and such books shall be open at all times to the inspection of any internal-revenue officer or agent.

New matter.

SEC. 42. That any producer of pure sweet wines, who is also a distiller, authorized to separate from fermented grape-juice, under internal-revenue laws, wine spirits, may use, free of tax, in the preparation of such sweet wines, under such regulations and after the filing of such notices and bonds, together with the keeping of such records and the rendition of such reports as to materials and products, as the Commissioner of Internal Revenue with the approval of the Secretary of the Treasury may prescribe, so much of such wine spirits so separated by him as may be necessary to fortify the wine for the preservation of the saccharine matter contained therein : *Provided*, That the wine spirits so used free of tax shall not be in excess of the amount required to introduce into such sweet wines in alcoholic strength equal to fourteen per centum of the volume of such wines after such use : *Provided further*, That such wine containing after such fortification more than twenty-four per centum of alcohol, as defined by section thirty-two hundred and forty-nine of the Revised Statutes, shall be forfeited to the United States : *Provided further*, That such use of wine spirits free from tax shall be confined to the months of August, September, October, November, December, January, February, March, and April of each year. The Commissioner of Internal Revenue, in determining the liability of any distiller of fermented grape-juice to assessment under section thirty-three hundred and nine of the Revised Statutes, is authorized to allow such distiller credit in his computation for the wine spirits used by him in preparing sweet wine under the provisions of this section.

New matter.

SEC. 43. That the wine spirits mentioned in section fifty-three of this act is the product resulting from the distillation of fermented grape juice, and shall be held to include the product commonly known as grape brandy; and the pure sweet wine which may be fortified free of tax, as provided in said section, is fermented grape-juice only, and shall contain no other substance of any kind whatever introduced before, at the time of, or after fermentation, and such sweet wine shall contain not less than four per centum of saccharine matter, which saccharine strength may be determined by testing, with Balling's saccharometer or must-scale, such sweet-wine, after the evaporation of the spirit contained therein, and restoring the sample tested to original volume by addition of water.

New matter.

SEC. 44. That any person who shall use wine spirits, as defined by section fifty-four of this act, or other spirits on which the internal-revenue tax has not been paid, otherwise than within the limitations set forth in section fifty-five of this act, and in accordance with the regulations made pursuant to this act, shall be liable to a penalty of double the amount of the tax on the wine spirits or other spirits so unlawfully used. Whenever it is impracticable in any case to ascertain the quantity of wine spirits or other spirits that have been used in violation of this act in mixtures with any wines, all alcohol contained in such unlawful mixtures of wine with wine spirits or other spirits in excess of ten per centum shall be held to be unlawfully used : *Provided, however*, That if water has been added to such unlawful mixtures, either before, at the time of, or after such unlawful use of wine-spirits or other spirits, all the alcohol contained therein shall be considered to have been unlawfully used. In reference to alcoholic strength of wines and mixtures of wines with spirits in this act the measurement is intended to be according to volume and not according to weight.

New matter.

SEC. 45. That under such regulations and official supervision, and upon the execution of such entries and the giving of such bonds, bills of lading, and other security as the Commissioner of Internal Revenue, with the approval of the Secretary of the Treasury, shall prescribe, any producer of pure sweet wines as defined by this act may withdraw wine spirits from any special bonded ware-house free of tax, in original packages, in any quantity not less than eighty wine-gallons, and may use so much of the same as may be required by him, under such regulations, and after the filing of such notices and bonds, and the keeping of such records, and the rendition of such reports as to materials and products and the disposition of the same as the Commissioner of Internal Revenue with the approval of the Secretary of the Treasury, shall prescribe, in fortifying the pure sweet wines made by him, and for no other purpose, in accordance with the limitations and provisions as to uses, amount to be used, and period for using the same set forth in section fifty-three of this act; and the Commissioner of Internal Revenue, with the approval of the Secretary of the Treasury, is authorized, whenever he shall deem it to be necessary for the prevention of violations of this law, to prescribe that wine-spirits withdrawn under this section shall not be used to fortify wines except at a certain distance prescribed by him from any distillery, rectifying-house, winery, or other establishment used for producing or storing distilled spirits, or for making or storing wines other than wines which are so fortified, and that in the building in which such fortification of wines.is practiced no wines or spirits other than those permitted by his regulation shall be stored. The use of wine-spirits free of tax for the fortification of sweet wines under this act shall be begun and completed at the vineyard of the wine-grower where the grapes are crushed and the grape juice is expressed and fermented, such use to be under the immediate supervision of an officer of internal revenue, who shall make returns describing the kinds and quantities of wine so fortified, and shall affix such stamps and seals to the packages containing such wines as may be prescribed by the Commissioner of Internal Revenue, with the approval of the Secretary of the Treasury; and the Commissioner of Internal Revenue shall provide by regulations the time within which wines so fortified with the wine spirits so withdrawn may be subject to inspection, and for final accounting for the use of such wine-spirits and for rewarehousing or for payment of the tax on any portion of such wine spirits which remain not used in fortifying pure sweet wines.

New matter.

SEC. 46. That wine-spirits may be withdrawn from special bonded warehouses at the instance of any person desiring to use the same to fortify any wines, in accordance with commercial demands of foreign markets, when such wines are intended for exportation, without the payment of tax on the amount of wine spirits used in such fortification, under such regulations, and after making such entries, and executing and filing with the collector of the district from which the removal is to be made such bonds and bills of lading, and giving such other additional security to prevent the use of such wine-spirits free of tax otherwise than in the fortification of wine intended for exportation, and for the due exportation of the wine so fortified, as may be prescribed by the Commissioner of Internal Revenue, with the approval of the Secretary of the Treasury; and all of the provisions of law governing the exportation of distilled spirits free of tax, so far as applicable, shall apply to the withdrawal and use of wine-spirits and the exportation of the same in accordance with this section; and the Commissioner of Internal Revenue is authorized, subject to approval by the Secretary of the Treasury, to prescribe that wine-spirits intended for the fortification of wines under this section shall not be introduced into such wines except under the immediate supervision of an officer of internal revenue, who shall make returns describing the kinds and quantities of wine so fortified, and shall affix such stamps and seals to the packages containing such wines as may be prescribed by the Commissioner of Internal Revenue, with the approval of the Secretary of the Treasury. Whenever such wine-spirits are withdrawn as provided herein for the fortification of wines intended for exportation by sea they shall be introduced into such wines only after removal from storage and arrival alongside of the vessel which is to transport the same; and whenever transportation of such wines is to be effected by land carriage the Commissioner of Internal Revenue, with the approval of the Secretary of the Treasury, shall prescribe such regulations as to sealing packages and vehicles containing the same, and as to the supervision of transportation from the point of departure, which point shall be determined as the place where such wine-spirits may be introduced into such wines to the point of destination as may be necessary to insure the due exportation of such fortified wines.

New matter.

SEC. 47. That all provisions of law relating to the re-importation of any goods of domestic growth or manufacture which were originally liable to an internal-revenue tax shall be, as far as applicable, enforced against any domestic wines sought to be re-imported; and duty shall be levied and collected upon the same when re-imported, as an original importation.

New matter.

SEC. 48. That any person using wine spirits or other spirits which have not been tax-paid in fortifying wine otherwise than as provided for in this act, shall be guilty of a misdemeanor, and shall, on conviction thereof, be punished for each offense by a fine of not more than two thousand dollars, and for every offense other than the first also by imprisonment for not more than one year.

SEC. 49, That wine spirits used in fortifying wines may be recovered from such wine only on the premises of a duly authorized grape-brandy distiller; and for the purpose of such recovery wines so fortified may be received as material on the premises of such a distiller, on a special permit of the collector of internal revenue in whose district the distillery is located; and the distiller will be held to pay the tax on a product from such wines as will include both the alcoholic strength therein produced by the fermentation of the grape-juice and that obtained from the added distilled spirits.

New matter.

SEC. 50. That on and after the day when this act shall go into effect all goods, wares, and merchandise previously imported, for which no entry has been made, and all goods, wares, and merchandise previously entered without payment of duty and under bond for warehousing, transportation, or any other purpose, for which no permit of delivery to the importer or his agent has been issued, shall be subjected to no other duty upon the entry or the withdrawal thereof than if the same were imported respectively after that day : *Provided*, That any imported merchandise deposited in bond in any public or private bonded warehouse having been so deposited prior to the first day of October, eighteen hundred and ninety, may be withdrawn for consumption at any time prior to February first, eighteen hundred and ninety-one, upon the payment of duties at the rates in force prior to the passage of this act : *Provided further*, That when duties are based upon the weight of merchandise deposited in any public or private bonded warehouse said duties shall be levied and collected upon the weight of such merchandise at the time of its withdrawal.

SEC. 51. That all goods, wares, articles, and merchandise manufactured wholly or in part in any foreign country by convict labor, shall not be entitled to entry at any of the ports of the United States, and the importation thereof is hereby prohibited, and the Secretary of the Treasury is authorized to prescribe such regulations as may be necessary for the enforcement of this provision.

New matter.

SEC. 52. That the value of foreign coin as expressed in the money of account of the United States shall be that of the pure metal of such coin of standard value ; and the values of the standard coins in circulation of the various nations of the world shall be estimated quarterly by the Director of the Mint, and be proclaimed by the Secretary of the Treasury immediately after the passage of this act and thereafter quarterly on the first day of January, April, July and October in each year.

Old law provided for annual estimation and proclamation.

SEC. 53. That all special taxes shall become due on the first day of July, eighteen hundred and ninety-one, and on the first day of July in each year thereafter, or on commencing any trade or business on which such tax is imposed. In the former case the tax shall be reckoned for one year ; and in the latter case it shall be reckoned proportionately, from the first day of the month in which the liability to a special tax commenced to the first day of July following. Special tax stamps may be issued for the months of May and June, eighteen hundred and ninety-one, upon payment of the amount of tax reckoned proportionately under the laws now in force, and such stamps which have been or may be issued for the period ending April thirtieth, eighteen hundred and ninety, may, upon payment of one-sixth of the amount required to be paid for such stamps for one year, be extended until July first, eighteen hundred and ninety-one, under such regulations as may be prescribed by the Commissioner of Internal Revenue. And it shall be the duty of special tax payers to render their returns to the deputy collector at such times within the calendar month in which the special tax liability commenced as shall enable him to receive such returns, duly signed and verified, not later than the last day of the month, except in case of sickness or absence, as provided for in section three thousand one hundred and seventy-six of the Revised Statutes.

SEC. 54. That section twenty of the act entitled "An act to simplify the laws in relation to the collection of revenues," approved June tenth, eighteen hundred and ninety, is hereby amended to read as follows :

"**Sec. 20.** That any merchandise deposited in bond in any public or private bonded-warehouse may be withdrawn for consumption within three years from the date of original importation, on payment of the duties and charges to which it may be subject by law at the time of such withdrawal: *Provided,* That nothing herein shall affect or impair existing provisions of law in regard to the disposal of perishable or explosive articles."

Sec. 55. That all laws and parts of laws inconsistent with this act are hereby repealed : *Provided, however,* That the repeal of existing laws, or modifications thereof, embraced in this act shall not affect any act done or any right accruing or accrued, or any suit or proceeding had or commenced in any civil cause before the said repeal or modifications, but all rights and liabilities under said laws shall continue and may be enforced in the same manner as if said repeal or modification had not been made.

Any offenses committed, and all penalties or forfeitures or liabilities incurred under any statute embraced in, or changed, modified, or repealed by this act may be prosecuted and punished, in the same manner and with the same effect as if this act had not been passed. All acts of limitation, whether applicable to civil causes and proceedings or to the prosecution of offenses, or for the recovery of penalties or forfeitures, embraced in, or modified, changed, or repealed by this act, shall not be affected thereby, and all suits, proceedings, or prosecutions, whether civil or criminal, for causes arrising or acts done or committed prior to the passage of this act may be commenced and prosecuted within the same time and with the same effect as if this act had not been passed.

Approved October 1st, 1890.

3695——8

ADMINISTRATIVE CUSTOMS LAW OF 1890,

WITH

SYNOPSIS OF CONTENTS.

SYNOPSIS OF CONTENTS.

117

An act to simplify the laws in relation to the collection of the revenues.

Be it enacted by the Senate and House of Representatives of the United States of America in Congress assembled, That all merchandise imported into the United States shall, for the purpose of this act, be deemed and held to be the property of the person to whom the merchandise may be consigned: but the holder of any bill of lading consigned to order and indorsed by the consignor shall be deemed the consignee thereof; and in case of the abandonment of any merchandise to the underwriters the latter may be recognized as the consignee.

SEC. 2. That all invoices of imported merchandise shall be made out in the currency of the place or country from whence the importations shall be made or if purchased in the currency actually paid therefor, shall contain a correct description of such merchandise, and shall be made in triplicate or in quadruplicate in case of merchandise intended for immediate transportation without appraisement, and signed by the person owning or shipping the same, if the merchandise has been actually purchased, or by the manufacturer or owner thereof, if the same has been procured otherwise than by purchase, or by the duly authorized agent of such purchaser, manufacturer, or owner.

SEC. 3. That all such invoices shall, at or before the shipment of the merchandise, be produced to the consul, vice consul, or commertial agent of the United States of the consular district in which the merchandise was manufactured or purchased as the case may be, for export to the United States, and shall have indorsed thereon, when so produced, a declaration signed by the purchaser, manufacturer, owner, or agent, setting forth that the invoice is in all respects correct and true, and was made at the place from which the merchandise is to be exported to the United States; that it contains, if the merchandise was obtained by purchase, a true and full statement of the time when, the place where, the person from whom the same was purchased, and the actual cost thereof and of all charges thereon, as provided by this act; and that no discounts, bounties, or drawbacks are contained in the invoice but such as have been actually allowed thereon; and when obtained in any other manner than by purchase, the actual market value or wholesale price thereof at the time of exportation to the United States in the principal markets of the country from whence exported; that such actual market value is the price at which the merchandise described in the invoice is freely offered for sale to all purchasers in said markets, and that it is the price which the manufacturer or owner making the declaration would have received, and was willing to receive, for such merchandise sold in the ordinary course of trade, in the usual wholesale quantities, and that it includes all charges thereon as provided by this act; and the actual quantity thereof; and that no different invoice of the merchandise mentioned in the invoice so produced has been or will be furnished to any one. If the merchandise was actually purchased, the declaration shall also contain a statement that the currency in which such invoice is made out is that which was actually paid for the merchandise by the purchaser.

SEC. 4. That, except in case of personal effects accompanying the passenger, no importation of any merchandise exceeding one hundred dollars in dutiable value shall be admitted to entry without the production of a duly-certified invoice thereof as required by law, or of an affidavit made by the owner, importer, or consignee, before the collector or his deputy, showing why it is impracticable to produce such invoice; and no entry shall be made in the absence of a certified invoice, upon affidavit as aforesaid, unless such affidavit be accompanied by a statement in the form of an invoice, or otherwise, showing the actual cost of such merchandise, if purchased, or if obtained otherwise than by purchase, the actual market value or wholesale price thereof at the time of exportation to the United States, in the principal markets of the country from which the same has been imported; which statement shall be verified by the oath of the owner, importer, consignee, or agent desiring to make entry of the merchandise, to be administered by the collector or his deputy, and it shall be lawful for the collector or his deputy to examine the deponent under oath touching the sources of his knowledge, information, or belief in the premises, and to require him to produce any letter, paper, or statement of account, in his possession, or under his control, which may assist the officers of customs in ascertaining the actual value of the importation or any part thereof; and in default of such production when so requested, such owner, importer, consignee, or agent shall be thereafter debarred from producing any such letter, paper, or statement for the purpose of avoiding any additional duty, penalty, or forfeiture incurred under this act, unless he shall show to the satisfaction of the court or the officers of the customs, as the case may be, that it was not in his power to produce the same when so demanded; and no merchandise shall be admitted to entry under the provisions of this section unless the collector shall be satisfied that the failure to produce a duly certified invoice is due to causes beyond the control of the owner, consignee, or agent thereof: *Provided*, That the Secretary of the Treasury may make regulations by which books, magazines, and other periodicals published and imported in successive parts, numbers, or volumes, and entitled to be imported free of duty, shall require but one declaration for the entire series. And when entry of merchandise exceeding one hundred dollars in value is made by a statement in the form of an invoice the collector shall require a bond for the production of a duly certified invoice.

SEC. 5. That whenever merchandise imported into the United States is entered by invoice, one of the following declarations, according to the nature of the case, shall be filed with the collector of the port, at the time of entry by the owner, importer, consignee, or agent; which declaration so filed shall be duly signed by the owner, importer, consignee, or agent, before the collector, or before a notary public or other officer duly authorized by law to administer oaths and take acknowledgments, who may be designated by the Secretary of the Treasury to receive such declarations and to certify to the identity of the persons making them, under regulations to be prescribed by the Secretary of the Treasury; and every officer so designated shall file with the collector of the port a copy of his official signature and seal: *Provided*. That if any of the invoices or bills of lading of any merchandise imported in any one vessel, which should otherwise be embraced in said entry, have not been received at the date of the entry, the declaration may state the fact, and thereupon such merchandise of which the invoices or bills of lading are not produced shall not be included in such entry, but may be entered subsequently.

DECLARATION OF CONSIGNEE, IMPORTER, OR AGENT.

I ———— ————, do solemnly and truly declare that I am the consignee [importer or agent] of the merchandise described in the annexed entry and invoice; that the invoice and bill of lading now presented by me to the collector of ———— ——— are the true and only invoice and bill of lading by me received of all the goods, wares, and merchandise imported in the ———— whereof ———— ———— is master, from ———— ————, for account of any person whomsoever for whom I am authorized to enter the same; that the said invoice and bill of lading are in the state in which they were actually received by me, and that I do not know or believe in the existence of any other invoice or bill of lading of the said goods, wares, and merchandise; that the entry now delivered to the collector contains a just and true account of the said goods, wares, and merchandise, according to the said invoice and bill of lading; that nothing has been, on my part, nor to my knowledge on the part of any other person, concealed or suppressed, whereby the United States may be defrauded of any part of the duty lawfully due on the said goods, wares, and merchandise; that the said invoice and the declaration therein are in all respects true, and were made by the person by whom the same purports to have been made; and that if at any time hereafter I discover any error in the said invoice, or in the account now rendered of the said goods, wares, and merchandise, or receive any other invoice of the same, I will immediately make the same known to the collector of this district. And I do further solemnly and truly declare that to the best of my knowledge and belief [insert the name and residence of the owner or owners] is [or are] the owner (or owners) of the goods, wares, and merchandise mentioned in the annexed entry; that the invoice now produced by me exhibits the actual cost (if purchased) or the actual market value or wholesale price (if otherwise obtained) at the time of exportation to the United States in the principal markets of the country from whence imported of the said goods, wares, and merchandise, and includes and specifies the value of all cartons, cases, crates, boxes, sacks, and coverings of any kind, and all other costs, charges, and expenses incident to placing said goods, wares, and merchandise in condition, packed ready for shipment to the United States, and no other or different discount, bounty, or drawback but such as has been actually allowed on the same.

DECLARATION OF OWNER IN CASES WHERE MERCHANDISE HAS BEEN ACTUALLY PURCHASED.

I, ———— ———— do solemnly and truly declare that I am the owner of the merchandise described in the annexed entry and invoice; that the entry now delivered by me to the collector of ———— contains a just and true account of all the goods, wares, and merchandise imported by or consigned to me, in the ———— ———— whereof ———— ———— is master, from ————; that the invoice and entry which I now produce contain a just and faithful account of the actual cost of the said goods, wares, and merchandise and include and specifies the value of all cartons, cases, crates, boxes, sacks, and coverings of any kind, and all other costs, charges, and expenses incident to placing said goods, wares, and merchandise in condition, packed ready for shipment to the United States, and no other discount, drawback, or bounty but such as has been actually allowed on the same; that I do not know nor believe in the existence of any invoice or bill of lading other than those now produced by me, and that they are in the state in which I actually received them. And I further solemnly and truly declare that I have not in the said entry or invoice concealed or suppressed anything whereby the United States may be defrauded of any part of the duty lawfully due on the said goods, wares, and merchandise; that to the best of my knowledge and belief the said invoice and the declaration thereon are in all respects true, and were made by the person by whom the same purports to have been made; and that if at any time hereafter I discover any error in the said invoice or in the account now produced of the said goods, wares, and merchandise, or receive any other invoice of the same, I will immediately make the same known to the collector of this district.

DECLARATION OF MANUFACTURER OR OWNER IN CASES WHERE MERCHANDISE HAS NOT BEEN ACTUALLY PURCHASED.

I, ———— ————, do solemnly and truly declare that I am the owner (or manufacturer) of the merchandise described in the annexed entry and invoice; that the entry now delivered by me to the collector of ——— contains a just and true account of all the goods, wares, and merchandise imported by or consigned to me in the ———, whereof ——— ——— is master, from ———; that the said goods, wares, and merchandise were not actually bought by me, or by my agent, in the ordinary mode of bargain and sale, but that nevertheless the invoice which I now produce contains a just and faithful valuation of the same, at their actual market value or wholesale price, at the time of exportation to the United States, in the principal markets of the country from whence imported for my account (or for account of myself or partners); that such actual market value is the price at which the merchandise described in the invoice is freely offered for sale to all purchasers in said markets, and is the price which I would have received and was willing to receive for such merchandise sold in the ordinary course of trade in the usual wholesale quantities; that the said invoice contains also a just and faithful account of all the cost of finishing said goods, wares, and merchandise to their present condition, and includes and specifies, the value of all cartons, cases, crates, boxes, sacks, and coverings of any kind, and all other costs and charges incident to placing said goods, wares, and merchandise in condition packed ready for shipment to the United States, and no other discount, drawback, or bounty but such as has been actually allowed on the said goods, wares, and merchandise; that the said invoice and the declaration thereon are in all respects true, and were made by the person by whom the same purports to have been made; that I do not know nor believe in the existence of any invoice or bill of lading other than those now produced by me, and that they are in the state in which I actually received them. And I do further solemnly and truly declare that I have not in the said entry or invoice concealed or suppressed anything whereby the United States may be defrauded of any part of the duty lawfully due on the said goods, wares, and merchandise; and that if at any time hereafter I discover any error in the said invoice, or in the account now produced of the said goods, wares, and merchandise, or receive any other invoice of the same, I will immediately make the same known to the collector of this district.

Sec. 6. That any person who shall knowingly make any false statement in the declarations provided for in the preceding section, or shall aid or procure the making of any such false statement as to any matter material thereto, shall, on conviction thereof, be punished by a fine not exceeding five thousand dollars, or by imprisonment at hard labor not more than two years, or both, in the discretion of the court : *Provided*, That nothing in this section shall be construed to relieve imported merchandise from forfeiture by reason of such false statement or for any cause elsewhere provided by law.

Sec. 7. That the owner, consignee, or agent of any imported merchandise which has been actually purchased, may, at the time when he shall make and verify his written entry of such merchandise, but not afterwards, make such addition in the entry to the cost or value given in the invoice, or pro forma invoice, or statement in form of an invoice, which he shall produce with his entry, as in his opinion may raise the same to the actual market value or wholesale price of such merchandise at the time of exportation to the United States, in the principal markets of the country from which the same has been imported ; but no such addition shall be made upon entry to the invoice value of any imported merchandise obtained otherwise than by actual purchase ; and the collector within whose district any merchandise may be imported or entered, whether the same has been actually purchased or procured otherwise than by purchase, shall cause the actual market value or wholesale price of such merchandise to be appraised ; and if the appraised value of any article of imported merchandise shall exceed by more than ten per centum the value declared in the entry, there shall be levied, collected, and paid, in addition to the duties imposed by law on such merchandise, a further sum equal to two per centum of the total appraised value for each one per centum that such appraised value exceeds the value declared in the entry ; and the additional duties shall only apply to the particular article or articles in each invoice which are undervalued ; and if such appraised value shall exceed the value declared in the entry more than forty per centum, such entry may be held to be presumptively fraudulent, and the collector of customs may seize such merchandise and proceed as in cases of forfeiture for violations of the customs laws ; and in any legal proceedings which may result from such seizure the fact of such undervaluation shall be presumptive evidence of fraud, and the burden of proof shall be on the claimant to rebut the same, and forfeiture shall be adjudged unless he shall rebut said presumption of fraudulent intent by sufficient evidence : *Provided*, That the forfeitures provided for in this section shall apply to the whole of the merchandise or the value thereof in the case or package containing the particular article or articles in each invoice which are undervalued : *And provided further*, That all additional duties, penalties, or forfeitures, applicable to merchandise entered by a duly certified invoice shall be alike applicable to goods entered by a pro forma invoice or statement in form of an invoice. The duty shall not, however, be assessed upon an amount less than the invoice or entered value.

Sec. 8. That when merchandise entered for customs duty has been consigned for sale by or on account of the manufacturer thereof, to a person, agent, partner, or consignee in the United States, such person, agent, partner, or consignee shall, at the time of the entry of such merchandise, present to the collector of customs at the port where such entry is made, as a part of such entry, and in addition to the certified invoice or statement in the form of an invoice required by law, a statement signed by such manufacturer, declaring the cost of production of such merchandise, such cost to include all the elements of cost as stated in section eleven of this act. When merchandise entered for customs duty has been consigned for sale by or on account of a person other than the manufacturer of such merchandise, to a person, agent, partner, or consignee in the United States, such person, agent, partner, or consignee shall at the time of the entry of such merchandise present to the collector of customs at the port where such entry is made, as a part of such entry, a statement signed by the consignor thereof, declaring that the merchandise was actually purchased by him or for his account, and showing the time when, the place where, and from whom he purchased the merchandise, and in detail the price he paid for the same: *Provided*, That the statements required by this section shall be made in triplicate, and shall bear the attestation of the consular officer of the United States resident within the consular district wherein the merchandise was manufactured, if consigned by the manufacturer or for his account, or from whence it was imported when consigned by a person other than the manufacturer, one copy thereof to be delivered to the person making the statement, one copy to be transmitted with the triplicate invoice of the merchandise to the collector of the port in the United States to which the merchandise is consigned, and the remaining copy to be filed in the consulate.

SEC. 9. That if any owner, importer, consignee, agent, or other person shall make or attempt to make any entry of imported merchandise by means of any fradulent or false invoice, affidavit, letter, paper, or by means of any false statement, written or verbal, or by means of any false or fradulent practice or appliance whatsoever, or shall be guilty of any willful act or omission by means whereof the United States shall be deprived of the lawful duties, or any portion thereof, accruing upon the merchandise, or any portion thereof, embraced or referred to in such invoice, affidavit, letter, paper, or statement, or affected by such act or omission, such merchandise, or the value thereof, to be recovered from the person making the entry, shall be forfeited, which forfeiture shall only apply to the whole of the merchandise or the value thereof in the case or package containing the particular article or articles of merchandise to which such fraud or false paper or statement relates; and such person shall, upon conviction, be fined for each offense a sum not exceeding five thousand dollars, or be imprisoned for a time not exceeding two years, or both, in the discretion of the court.

SEC. 10. That it shall be the duty of the appraisers of the United States, and every of them, and every person who shall act as such appraiser, or of the collector, as the case may be, by all reasonable ways and means in his or their power to ascertain, estimate, and appraise (any invoice or affidavit thereto or statement of cost, or of cost of production to the contrary notwithstanding) the actual market value and wholesale price of the merchandise at the time of exportation to the United States, in the principal markets of the country whence the same has been imported, and the number of yards, parcels, or quantities, and actual market value or wholesale price of every of them, as the case may require.

SEC. 11. That when the actual market value, as herein defined, of any article of imported merchandise wholly or partially manufactured and subject to ad valorem duty, or to duty based in whole or in part on value, can not be ascertained to the satisfaction of the appraising officer, the appraiser or appraisers shall use all available means to ascertain the cost of production of such merchandise at the time of exportation to the United States, and at the place of manufacture; such cost of production to include cost of materials and of fabrication, all general expenses covering each and every outlay of whatsoever nature incident to such production, together with the expense of preparing and putting up such merchandise ready for shipment, and an addition of eight per cent. upon the total cost as thus ascertained; and in no such case shall such merchandise be appraised upon original appraisal or re-appraisement at less than the total cost of production as thus ascertained.

SEC. 12. That there shall be appointed by the President, by and with the advice and consent of the Senate, nine general appraisers of merchandise, each of whom shall receive a salary of seven thousand dollars a year. Not more than five of such general appraisers shall be appointed from the same political party. They shall not be engaged in any other business, avocation, or employment, and may be removed from office at any time by the President for inefficiency, neglect of duty, or malfeasance in office. They shall be employed at such ports and within such territorial limits, as the Secretary of the Treasury may from time to time prescribe, and are hereby authorized to exercise the powers, and duties devolved upon them by this act and to exercise, under the general direction of the Secretary of the Treasury, such other supervision over appraisements and classifications, for duty, of imported merchandise as may be needful to secure lawful and uniform appraisements and classifications at the several ports. Three of the general appraisers shall be on duty as a board of general appraisers daily (except Sunday and legal holidays) at the port of New York, during the business hours prescribed by the Secretary of the Treasury, at which port a place for samples shall be provided, under such rules and regulations as the Secretary of the Treasury may from time to time prescribe, which shall include rules as to the classes of articles to be deposited, the time of their retention, and as to their disposition, which place of samples shall be under the immediate control and direction of the board of general appraisers on duty at said port.

SEC. 13. That the appraiser shall revise and correct the reports of the assistant appraisers as he may judge proper, and the appraiser, or, at ports where there is no appraiser, the person acting as such, shall report to the collector his decision as to the value of the merchandise appraised. At ports where there is no appraiser, the certificate of the customs officer to whom is committed the estimating and collection of duties, of the dutiable value of any merchandise required to be appraised, shall be deemed and taken to be the appraisement of such merchandise. If the collector shall deem the appraisement of any imported merchandise too low he may order a reappraisement, which shall be made by one of the general appraisers, or, if the importer, owner, agent, or consignee of such merchandise shall be dissatisfied with the appraisement thereof, and shall have complied with the requirements of law with respect to the entry and appraisement of merchandise, he may, within two days thereafter give notice to the collector, in writing, of such dissatisfaction, on the receipt of which the collector shall at once direct a reappraisement of such merchandise by one of the general appraisers. The decision of the appraiser or the person acting as such (in cases where no objection is made thereto, either by the collector or by the importer, owner, consignee, or agent), or of the general appraiser in cases of re-appraisement, shall be final and conclusive as to the dutiable value of such merchandise against all parties interested therein, unless the importer, owner, consignee, or agent of the merchandise shall be dissatisfied with such decision, and shall, within two days thereafter give notice to the collector in writing of such dissatisfaction, or unless the collector shall deem the appraisement of the merchandise too low, in either case the collector shall transmit the invoice and all the papers appertaining thereto to the board of three general appraisers, which shall be on duty at the port of New York, or to a board of three general appraisers who may be designated by the Secretary of the Treasury for such duty at that port or at any other port, which board shall examine and decide the case thus submitted, and their decision, or that of a majority of them, shall be final and conclusive as to the dutiable value of such merchandise against all parties interested therein, and the collector or the person acting as such shall ascertain, fix, and liquidate the rate and amount of duties to be paid on such merchandise, and the dutiable costs and charges thereon, according to law.

SEC. 14. That the decision of the collector as to the rate and amount of duties chargeable upon imported merchandise, including all dutiable costs and charges, and as to all fees and exactions of whatever character (except duties on tonnage), shall be final and conclusive against all persons interested therein, unless the owner, importer, consignee, or agent of such merchandise, or the person paying such fees, charges, and exactions other than duties, shall, within ten days after "but not before" such ascertainment and liquidation of duties, as well in cases of merchandise entered in bond as for consumption, or within ten days after the payment of such fees, charges, and exactions, if dissatisfied with such decision give notice in writing to the collector, setting forth therein distinctly and specifically, and in respect to each entry or payment, the reasons for his objections thereto, and if the merchandise is entered for consumption shall pay the full amount of the duties and charges ascertained to be due thereon. Upon such notice and payment the collector shall transmit the invoice and all the papers and exhibits connected therewith to the board of three general appraisers, which shall be on duty at the port of New York, or to a board of three general appraisers who may be designated by the Secretary of the Treasury for such duty at that port or at any other port, which board shall examine and decide the case thus submitted, and their decision, or that of a majority of them, shall be final and conclusive upon all persons interested therein, and the record shall be transmitted to the proper collector or person acting as such who shall liquidate the entry accordingly, except in cases where an application shall be filed in the circuit court within the time and in the manner provided for in section fifteen of this act.

SEC. 15. That if the owner, importer, consignee, or agent of any imported merchandise, or the collector, or the Secretary of the Treasury, shall be dissatisfied with the decision of the board of general appraisers, as provided for in section fourteen of this act, as to the construction of the law and the facts respecting the classification of such merchandise and the rate of duty imposed thereon under such classification, they or either of them, may, within thirty days next after such decision, and not afterwards, apply to the circuit court of the United States within the district in which the matter arises, for a review of the questions of law and fact involved in such decision. Such application shall be made by filing in the office of the clerk of said circuit court a concise statement of the errors of law and fact complained of, and a copy of such statement shall be served on the collector, or on the importer, owner, consignee, or agent, as the case may be. Thereupon the court shall order the board of appraisers to return to said circuit court the record and the evidence taken by them, together with a certified statement of the facts involved in the case, and their decisions thereon; and all the evidence taken by and before said appraisers shall be competent evidence before said circuit court; and within twenty days after the aforesaid return is made the court may, upon the application of the Secretary of the Treasury, the collector of the port, or the importer, owner, consignee, or agent, as the case may be, refer it to one of said general appraisers, as an officer of the court, to take and return to the court such further evidence as may be offered by the Secretary of the Treasury, collector, importer, owner, consignee, or agent, within sixty days thereafter, in such order and under such rules as the court may prescribe; and such further evidence with the aforesaid returns shall constitute the record upon which said circuit court shall give priority to and proceed to hear and determine the questions of law and fact involved in such decision, respecting the classification of such merchandise and the rate of duty imposed thereon under such classification, and the decision of such court shall be final, and the proper collector, or person acting as such, shall liquidate the entry accordingly, unless such court shall be of opinion that the question involved is of such importance as to require a review of such decision by the Supreme Court of the United States, in which case said circuit court, or the judge making the decision may, within thirty days thereafter, allow an appeal to said Supreme Court; but an appeal shall be allowed on the part of the United States whenever the Attorney-General shall apply for it within thirty days after the rendition of such decision. On such original application, and on any such appeal, security for damages and costs shall be given as in the case of other appeals in cases in which the United States is a party. Said Supreme Court shall have jurisdiction and power to review such decision, and shall give priority to such cases, and may affirm, modify, or reverse such decision of such circuit court, and remand the case with such orders as may seem to it proper in the premises, which shall be executed accordingly. All final judgments, when in favor of the importer, shall be satisfied and paid by the Secretary of the Treasury from the permanent indefinite appropriation provided for in section twenty-three of this act. For the purposes of this section the circuit courts of the United States shall be deemed always open, and said circuit courts, respectively, may establish, and from time to time alter, rules and regulations not inconsistent herewith for the procedure in such cases as they shall deem proper.

SEC. 16. That the general appraisers, or any of them, are hereby authorized to administer oaths, and said general appraisers, the boards of general appraisers, the local appraisers or the collectors, as the case may be, may cite to appear before them, and examine upon oath any owner, importer, agent, consignee, or other person touching any matter or thing which they, or either of them, may deem material respecting any imported merchandise, in ascertaining the dutiable value or classification thereof ; and they, or either of them, may require the production of any letters, accounts, or invoices relating to said merchandise, and may require such testimony to be reduced to writing, and when so taken it shall be filed in the office of the collector, and preserved for use or reference until the final decision of the collector or said board of appraisers shall be made respecting the valuation or classification of said merchandise, as the case may be.

SEC. 17. That if any person so cited to appear shall neglect or refuse to attend, or shall decline to answer, or shall refuse to answer in writing any interrogatories, and subscribe his name to his deposition, or to produce such papers, when so required by a general appraiser, or a board of general appraisers, or a local appraiser or a collector, he shall be liable to a penalty of one hundred dollars ; and if such person be the owner, importer, or consignee, the appraisement which the general appraiser, or board of general appraisers, or local appraiser, or collector, where there is no appraiser, may make of the merchandise, shall be final and conclusive ; and any person who shall willfully and corruptly swear falsely on an examination before any general appraiser, or board of general appraisers, or local appraiser, or collector, shall be deemed guilty of perjury ; and if he is the owner, importer, or consignee, the merchandise shall be forfeited.

SEC. 18. That all decisions of the general appraisers and of the boards of general appraisers, respecting values and rates of duty, shall be preserved and filed, and shall be open to inspection under proper regulations to be prescribed by the Secretary of the Treasury. All decisions of the general appraisers shall be reported forthwith to the Secretary of the Treasury and to the board of general appraisers on duty at the port of New York, and the report to the board shall be accompanied, whenever practicable, by samples of the merchandise in question, and it shall be the duty of the said board, under the direction of the Secretary of the Treasury, to cause an abstract to be made and published of such decisions of the appraisers as they may deem important, and of the decisions of each of the general appraisers and boards of general appraisers, which abstract shall contain a general description of the merchandise in question, and of the value and rate of duty fixed in each case, with reference, whenever practicable, by number or other designation, to samples deposited in the place of samples at New York, and such abstract shall be issued from time to time, at least once in each week, for the information of customs officers and the public.

SEC. 19. That whenever imported merchandise is subject to an ad valorem rate of duty, or to a duty based upon or regulated in any manner by the value thereof, the duty shall be assessed upon the actual market value or wholesale price of such merchandise as bought and sold in usual wholesale quantities, at the time of exportation to the United States, in the principal markets of the country from whence imported, and in the condition in which such merchandise is there bought and sold for exportation to the United States, or consigned to the United States for sale, including the value of all cartons, cases, crates, boxes, sacks, and coverings of any kind, and all other costs, charges, and expenses incident to placing the merchandise in condition, packed ready for shipment to the United States, and if there be used for covering or holding imported merchandise, whether dutiable or free, any unusual article or form designed for use otherwise than in the bona fide transportation of such merchandise to the United States, additional duty shall be levied and collected upon such material or article at the rate to which the same would be subject if separately imported. That the words "value" or "actual market value" whenever used in this act or in any law relating to the appraisement of imported merchandise shall be construed to mean the actual market value or wholesale price as defined in this section.

SEC. 20. Any merchandise deposited in any public or private bonded-warehouse may be withdrawn for consumption within three years from the date of original importation, on payment of the duties and charges to which it may be subject by law at the time of such withdrawal: *Provided*, That nothing herein shall affect or impair existing provisions of law in regard to the disposal of perishable or explosive articles.

SEC. 21. That in all suits or informations brought, where any seizure has been made pursuant to any act providing for or regulating the collection of duties on imports or tonnage, if the property is claimed by any person, the burden of proof shall lie upon such claimant: *Provided*, That probable cause is shown for such prosecution, to be judged of by the court.

SEC. 22. That all fees exacted and oaths administered by officers of the customs, except as provided in this act, under or by virtue of existing laws of the United States, upon the entry of imported goods and the passing thereof through the customs, and also upon all entries of domestic goods, wares, and merchandise for exportation, be, and the same are hereby, abolished; and in case of entry of merchandise for exportation, a declaration, in lieu of an oath, shall be filed, in such form and under such regulations as may be prescribed by the Secretary of the Treasury; and the penalties provided in the sixth section of this act for false statements in such declaration shall be applicable to declarations made under this section: *Provided*, That where such fees, under existing laws, constitute, in whole or in part, the compensation of any officer, such officer shall receive, from and after the passage of this act, a fixed sum for each year equal to the amount which he would have been entitled to receive as fees for such services during said year.

SEC. 23. That no allowance for damage to goods, wares, and merchandise imported into the United States shall hereafter be made in the estimation and liquidation of duties thereon; but the importer thereof may, within ten days after entry, abandon to the United States all or any portion of goods, wares, and merchandise included in any invoice, and be relieved from the payment of the duties on the portion so abandoned: *Provided*, That the portion so abandoned shall amount to ten per centum or over of the total value or quantity of the invoice; and the property so abandoned shall be sold by public auction or otherwise disposed of for the account and credit of the United States under such regulations as the Secretary of the Treasury may prescribe.

SEC. 24. That whenever it shall be shown to the satisfaction of the Secretary of the Treasury that, in any case of unascertained or estimated duties, or payments made upon appeal, more money has been paid to or deposited with a collector of customs than, as has been ascertained by final liquidation thereof, the law required to be paid or deposited, the Secretary of the Treasury shall direct the Treasurer to refund and pay the same out of any money in the Treasury not otherwise appropriated. The necessary moneys therefor are hereby appropriated, and this appropriation shall be deemed a permanent indefinite appropriation; and the Secretary of the Treasury is hereby authorized to correct manifest clerical errors in any entry or liquidation, for or against the United States, at any time within one year of the date of such entry, but not afterwards: *Provided*, That the Secretary of the Treasury shall in his annual report to Congress, give a detailed statement of the various sums of money refunded under the provisions of this act or of any other act of Congress relating to the revenue, together with copies of the rulings under which repayments were made.

SEC. 25. That from and after the taking effect of this act no collector or other officer of the customs shall be in any way liable to any owner, importer, consignee, or agent of any merchandise, or any other person, for or on account of any rulings or decisions as to the classification of said merchandise or the duties charged thereon, or the collection of any dues, charges, or duties on or on account of said merchandise, or any other matter or thing as to which said owner, importer, consignee, or agent of such merchandise might, under this act, be entitled to appeal from the decision of said collector or other officer, or from any board of appraisers provided for in this act.

SEC. 26. That any person who shall give, or offer to give or promise to give any money or thing of value, directly or indirectly, to any officer or employee of the United States in consideration of or for any act or omission contrary to law in connection with or pertaining to the importation, appraisement, entry, examination, or inspection of goods, wares, or merchandise including herein any baggage, or of the liquidation of the entry thereof, or shall by threats or demands, or promises of any character attempt to improperly influence or control any such officer or employee of the United States as to the performance of his official duties shall, on conviction thereof, be fined not exceeding two thousand dollars, or be imprisoned at hard labor not more than one year, or both, in the discretion of the court; and evidence of such giving, or offering, or promising to give, satisfactory to the court in which such trial is had, shall be regarded as prima facie evidence that such giving or offering or promising was contrary to law, and shall put upon the accused the burden of proving that such act was innocent, and not done with an unlawful intention.

SEC. 27. That any officer or employee of the United States who shall, excepting for lawful duties or fees, solicit, demand, exact or receive from any person, directly or indirectly, any money or thing of value, in connection with or pertaining to the importation, appraisement, entry, examination, or inspection of goods, wares, or merchandise, including herein any baggage, or liquidation of the entry thereof, on conviction thereof, shall be fined not exceeding five thousand dollars, or be imprisoned at hard labor not more than two years, or both, in the discretion of the court. And evidence of such soliciting, demanding, exacting, or receiving, satisfactory to the court in which such trial is had, shall be regarded as prima facie evidence that such soliciting, demanding, exacting, or receiving was contrary to law, and shall put upon the accused the burden of proving that such act was innocent and not with an unlawful intention.

Sec. 28. That any baggage or personal effects arriving in the United States in transit to any foreign country may be delivered by the parties having it in charge to the collector of the proper district, to be by him retained, without the payment or exaction of any import duty, or to be forwarded by such collector to the collector of the port of departure and to be delivered to such parties on their departure for their foreign destination, under such rules and regulations as the Secretary of the Treasury may prescribe.

Sec. 29. That sections twenty-six hundred and eight, twenty-eight hundred and thirty-eight, twenty-eight hundred and thirty-nine, twenty-eight hundred and forty-one, twenty-eight hundred and forty-three, twenty-eight hundred and forty-five, twenty-eight hundred and fifty-three, twenty-eight hundred and fifty-four, twenty-eight hundred and fifty-six, twenty-eight hundred and fifty-eight, twenty-eight hundred and sixty, twenty-nine hundred, and twenty-nine hundred and two, twenty-nine hundred and five, twenty-nine hundred and seven, twenty-nine hundred and eight, twenty-nine hundred and nine, twenty-nine hundred and twenty-two, twenty-nine hundred and twenty-three, twenty-nine hundred and twenty-four, twenty-nine hundred and twenty-seven, twenty-nine hundred and twenty-nine, twenty-nine hundred and thirty, twenty-nine hundred and thirty-one, twenty-nine hundred and thirty-two, twenty-nine hundred and forty-three, twenty-nine hundred and forty-five, twenty-nine hundred and fifty-two, three thousand and eleven, three thousand and twelve, three thousand and twelve and one half, three thousand and thirteen, of the Revised Statutes of the United States, be, and the same are hereby, repealed, and sections nine, ten, eleven, twelve, fourteen, and sixteen of an act entitled "An act to amend the customs-revenue laws and to repeal moieties," approved June twenty-second, eighteen hundred and seventy-four, and sections seven, eight, and nine of the act entitled "An act to reduce internal-revenue taxation, and for other purposes," approved March third, eighteen hundred and eighty-three, and all other acts and parts of acts inconsistent with the provisions of this act, are hereby repealed, but the repeal of existing laws or modifications thereof embraced in this act shall not affect any act done, or any right accruing or accrued, or any suit or proceeding had or commenced in any civil cause before the said repeal or modifications; but all rights and liabilities under said laws shall continue and may be enforced in the same manner as if said repeal or modifications had not been made. Any offenses committed, and all penalties or forfeitures or liabilities incurred prior to the passage of this act under any statute embraced in or changed, modified, or repealed by this act may be prosecuted and punished in the same manner and with the same effect as if this act had not been passed. All acts of limitation, whether applicable to civil causes and proceedings or to the prosecution of offenses or for the recovery of penalties or forfeitures embraced in or modified, changed, or repealed by this act, shall not be affected thereby; and all suits, proceedings, or prosecutions, whether civil or criminal, for causes arising or acts done or committed prior to the passage of this act, may be commenced and prosecuted within the same time and with the same effect as if this act had not been passed. And provided further, That nothing in this act shall be construed to repeal the provisions of section three thousand and fifty-eight of the Revised Statutes as amended by the act approved February twenty-third, eighteen hundred and eighty-seven, in respect to the abandonment of merchandise to underwriters or the salvors of property, and the ascertainment of duties thereon.

SEC. 30. That this act shall take effect on the first day of August, eighteen hundred and ninety, except so much of section twelve as provides for the appointment of nine general appraisers, which shall take effect immediately.

Approved, June 10, 1890.

o

www.ingramcontent.com/pod-product-compliance
Lightning Source LLC
Chambersburg PA
CBHW031439280326
41927CB00038B/1132